Social Work
Practice

Transforming Social Work Practice – titles in the series

Applied Psychology for Social Work	ISBN 13 978 1 84445 071 8
Collaborative Social Work Practice	ISBN 13 978 1 84445 014 5
Communication and Interpersonal Skills in Social Work	ISBN 13 978 1 84445 019 0
Effective Practice Learning in Social Work	ISBN 13 978 1 84445 015 2
Management and Organisations in Social Work	ISBN 13 978 1 84445 044 2
Practical Computer Skills for Social Work	ISBN 13 978 1 84445 060 2
Social Work and Human Development (second edition)	ISBN 13 978 1 84445 112 8
Social Work and Mental Health (second edition)	ISBN 13 978 1 84445 068 8
Social Work in Education and Children's Services	ISBN 13 978 1 84445 045 9
Social Work Practice: Assessment, Planning, Intervention and Review (second edition)	ISBN 13 978 1 84445 113 5
Social Work with Children and Families	ISBN 13 978 1 84445 018 3
Social Work with Children, Young People and their Families in Scotland	ISBN 13 978 1 84445 031 2
Social Work with Drug and Substance Misusers	ISBN 13 978 1 84445 058 9
Social Work with Older People	ISBN 13 978 1 84445 017 6
Social Work with People with Learning Difficulties	ISBN 13 978 1 84445 042 8
Using the Law in Social Work (third edition)	ISBN 13 978 1 84445 114 2
Values and Ethics in Social Work Practice	ISBN 13 978 1 84445 067 1
What is Social Work? Context and Perspectives (second edition)	ISBN 13 978 1 84445 051 0
Youth Justice and Social Work	ISBN 13 978 1 84445 066 4

To order, please contact our distributor: BEBC Distribution, Albion Close, Parkstone, Poole, BH12 3LL. Telephone: 0845 230 9000, email: **learningmatters@bebc.co.uk**. You can also find more information on each of these titles and our other learning resources at **www.learningmatters.co.uk**

Social Work Practice:

Assessment, Planning, Intervention and Review

Second Edition

JONATHAN PARKER AND GRETA BRADLEY

Series Editors: Jonathan Parker and Greta Bradley

First published in 2003 by Learning Matters Ltd.

Reprinted in 2003, 2004 (twice), 2005 (twice) and 2006

Second edition in 2007

British Library Cataloguing in Publication Data
A CIP record for this book is available from the British Library.

ISBN-13: 978 1 84445 113 5

Cover and text design by Code 5 Design Associates Ltd
Project management by Deer Park Productions
Typeset by Pantek Arts Ltd, Maidstone, Kent
Printed and bound in Great Britain by Bell & Bain Ltd, Glasgow

Learning Matters Ltd
33 Southernhay East
Exeter EX1 1NX
Tel: 01392 215560
info@learningmatters.co.uk
www.learningmatters.co.uk

Contents

Introduction   vii

1 Understanding assessment in social work practice   1

2 Tools and diagrammatic aids to assessment   40

3 Developing, making and writing plans for
       effective social work   63

4 Intervening to make a difference   84

5 Reviews and the evaluation of practice   116

Conclusion   139

References   141

Index   149

Acknowledgements

We offer our heartfelt thanks to those friends, family and colleagues who have supported us during the preparation of the second edition of this book. We are also grateful to our students, past and present, and to colleagues who have offered criticism and made suggestions that have helped frame our revisions although, of course, responsibility for the changes must remain with us. Finally, we would like to thank the staff at Learning Matters for their on-going support and continued faith in the *Transforming Social Work Practice* series.

Introduction

This book is written for student social workers following a qualifying programme who are beginning to develop their skills and understanding of the knowledge and value requirements for practice. Whilst it is primarily aimed at students in their first year or level of study, it will be useful for subsequent years depending on how your programme is designed, what you are studying and especially as you move into practice learning in an agency setting. The book will also appeal to people considering a career in social work or social care but not yet studying for a social work degree as it will introduce you to some of the ways in which social workers practise. Perhaps you are studying for a health and social care foundation degree, Access to Higher Education programme or similar. It will assist students undertaking a range of social and health care courses in further education by providing a glimpse of the social work role and some of the methods used. Nurses, occupational therapists and other health and social care professionals will be able to gain an insight into the new requirements demanded of social workers. Experienced and qualified social workers, especially those contributing to practice learning, will also be able to use this book for consultation, teaching, revision and to gain an insight into the expectations raised by the qualifying degree in social work.

Requirements for social work education

During the first part of this century, social work education has undergone a major transformation to ensure that qualified social workers are educated at least to honours degree level and develop knowledge, skills and values which are common and shared. A vision for social work operating in complex human situations has been adopted. This is reflected in the following definition from the International Association of Schools of Social Work and International Federation of Social Workers, 2001:

> The social work profession promotes social change, problem solving in human relationships and the empowerment and liberation of people to enhance well-being. Utilising theories of human behaviour and social systems, social work intervenes at the points where people interact with their environments. Principles of human rights and social justice are fundamental to social work.

Whilst there is a great deal packed into this short and pithy definition it encapsulates the notion that social work concerns individual people and wider society. Social workers work with people who are vulnerable, who are struggling in some way to participate fully in society. Social workers walk that tightrope between individuals excluded from taking a place within society and the social and political environment that may have contributed to their marginalisation.

Social workers need to be highly skilled and knowledgeable to work effectively in this context and successive government ministers have been keen for social work education and practice to improve. In order to improve the quality of both these aspects of professional social work, it is crucial that you, as a student social worker, develop a rigorous grounding in and understanding of theories and models for social work. Such knowledge helps social workers to know what to do, when to do it and how to do it, whilst recognising that social work is a complex activity with no absolute 'rights' and 'wrongs' of practice for each situation. We agree with the minister responsible for developing the current qualifying award in championing the practical focus of social work, of being able to apply our knowledge to help others although not, perhaps, with the somewhat naïve and anti-intellectual stance implied.

> *Social work is a very* practical *job. It is about protecting people and changing their lives, not about being able to give a fluent and theoretical explanation of why they got into difficulties in the first place. New degree courses must ensure that theory and research directly informs and supports practice.*
>
> *The Requirements for Social Work Training set out the minimum standards for entry to social work degree courses and for the teaching and assessment that social work students must receive. The new degree will require social workers to demonstrate their practical application of skills and knowledge and their ability to solve problems and provide hope for people relying on social services for support.*
> (Jacqui Smith, Minister of Health, 2002)

The book aims to meet the learning needs outlined in the Department of Health's prescribed curriculum for competence in assessment, planning, intervention and review, incorporating the necessary knowledge, skills and the development of values.

The book will meet subject skills identified in the Quality Assurance Agency academic benchmark criteria for social work. These include understanding the nature of social work and developing problem-solving skills under the following four headings:

- managing problem-solving activities;

- gathering information (including searches and presentation of findings);

- analysis and synthesis;

- intervention and evaluation.

This approach will draw on and rely on you to acquire high quality communication skills, skills in working with others, and reflective skills in personal and professional development.

The book will also meet the National Occupational Standards (NOS) set for social workers. The Standards state clearly that operational process skills are central to competence. In the language of the NOS social workers must:

- prepare for work with people and assess their needs and circumstances;

- plan, carry out, review and evaluate in social work;

- support individuals to represent needs, views and circumstances;

- manage risk;

- be accountable with supervision and support for own practice;

- demonstrate professional competence in social work practice.

In essence, the book will concentrate on models that are current in practice and transferable across settings. These models are active and practical and are open to evaluation. Case studies, which focus predominantly on work with children and families and older people, will be used throughout to enhance this process and to illustrate key points. In doing so we will necessarily omit several areas of social work practice. We have deliberately limited our focus to two service user groups that of children and families and older people. We refer readers with different subject interests to other texts in the series, such as Golightley's (2006) *Social Work and Mental Health* (second edition) or William's (2006) *Social Work with People with Learning Difficulties.*

Book structure

Research indicates that social workers vary considerably in the extent that they make and test hypotheses in practice (Sheppard, Newstead, DiCaccavo and Ryan, 2001). A shift towards understanding 'knowledge as process' as opposed to 'knowledge as product' is suggested as one way to integrate theory and practice. This means seeing knowledge as something that develops by your active involvement in using it rather than being given a set of instructions and understanding developed by others. These changes to social work education and the implementation of new degree courses mean that there is a need for new, practical learning support material to help you achieve the qualification. This book is designed to help you gain knowledge concerning assessment, planning, intervention and review, to reflect on that knowledge and apply it in practice. The emphasis in this book concerns you achieving the requirements of the curriculum and developing knowledge that will assist you in meeting the occupational standards for social work.

The book has five main chapters covering assessment, assessment tools, planning, intervention and review and evaluation of practice. In the first chapter you will be introduced to assessment in social work and will explore what an assessment means for social workers and the people with whom they work. Key issues in respect of ethics, power, professionalism in social work and anti-oppressive practice will also be discussed. You will examine different models and types of assessment and look in detail at two aspects of contemporary practice that demand good assessment skills: working with children and families and community care, care management and the single assessment process.

Chapter 2 continues the theme of assessment. Here you will learn about and develop a practical understanding of a range of practical tools designed to help in making assessments. Whilst assessments are not simply information gathering exercises and are jointly constructed ventures undertaken with service users, a certain amount of information is crucial. By gaining an understanding of family stories and histories (genograms), people, organisations and agencies important to service users (ecomaps), cultural issues (cultura-grams), and the individual's perceptions of important life events (life road maps and flow charts), you will begin to develop useful techniques for undertaking assessments.

In Chapter 3 you will consider how an assessment leads social workers to develop and write clear plans for work with service users and carers. This chapter will provide an introduction to the construction of plans and some key issues to be taken into account when formulating them. In making plans, students will be asked to consider the effects of working with other professions and with informal carers and service users. Contemporary guidance and advice on care planning will be provided and activities will help you to forge links between knowledge and practice. A particular focus will concern the writing of care plans and the importance of accessibility and involvement to make plans effective. How plans can be person-focused and proactive in achieving agreed aims and in charting a course for intervention will link to Chapter 4.

In Chapter 4 you will explore ways of intervening in social work to implement plans made and to achieve agreed goals. The chapter will introduce a number of important and commonly used models for social work practice. These will be applied to case study material. Current guidance, research and advice on intervening effectively will be provided and the activities will help you to make links between knowledge and practice. You will be asked to question the purpose and use of intervention, especially in respect of care and control issues. You will explore and reflect on the use of power and authority to protect or when working with people who do not want to see you.

The fifth chapter concerns the final stage of the social work process, reviewing what has been achieved. Student social workers, and experienced practitioners, often have many anxieties about reviewing and evaluating their work in a systematic way. In an effective review and evaluation of work undertaken, practice is subject to scrutiny and outcomes and objectives are measured. Whilst this can be a somewhat daunting process, it emphasises accountability and allows practitioners to develop knowledge and skills in determining what works in which circumstances. In these days of increased accountability and audit it is essential that social workers evaluate their practice. This can have the added bonus of ensuring that your practice is refined to achieve agreed goals and that social work is promoted as effective to other professions and the wider public. In this chapter you will explore the importance of formal reviews and a number of ways of evaluating social work practice.

Concluding remarks and signposts will be offered at the end of the book. At this stage you will be invited to review the learning outcomes set for the chapters. You will be encouraged to chart and monitor your learning, taking developmental needs and reflections forward to other books within the series.

Learning features

The book is interactive. You are encouraged to work through the book as an active participant, taking responsibility for your learning, in order to increase your knowledge, understanding and ability to apply this learning to practice. You will be expected to reflect creatively on how immediate learning needs can be met in the area of assessment, planning, intervention and review and how your professional learning can be developed in your future career.

What do we mean by reflection? Whilst it is a much used term it is often left undefined which can lead to confusion, Parker (2004). What we mean follows. There are a number of case studies throughout the book that will help you to examine theories and models for social work practice. We have devised activities that require you to reflect on experiences, situations and events and help you to review and summarise learning undertaken. In this way your knowledge will become deeply embedded as part of your development. When you come to practice learning in an agency, the work and reflection undertaken here will help you to improve and hone your skills and knowledge.

This book will introduce knowledge and learning activities for you as a student social worker concerning some of the central processes relating to issues of daily practice in all areas of the discipline. Suggestions for further reading will be made at the end of each chapter.

Professional development and reflective practice

Great emphasis is placed on developing skills of reflection about, in and on practice. This has developed over many years in social work. It is important also that you reflect prior to practice, as this emphasis on a thoughtful and planned approach will help you make your work clear to service users and also more open to review, so you can improve your practice in the future. This book will assist you in developing a questioning approach that looks in a critical way at your thoughts, experiences and practice and seeks to heighten your skills in refining your practice as a result. Reflection is central to good social work practice, but only if action results from that reflection.

Reflecting about, in and on your practice is not only important during your education to become a social worker, it is considered key to continued professional development. As we move to a profession that acknowledges life-long learning as a way of keeping up-to-date, ensuring that research informs practice and striving continually to improve skills and values for practice, it is important to begin the process at the outset of your development. The importance of professional development is clearly shown by its inclusion in the National Occupational Standards and reflected in the General Social Care Council (GSCC) *Code of practice for employees*.

Chapter 1
Understanding assessment in social work practice

A C H I E V I N G   A   S O C I A L   W O R K   D E G R E E

This chapter will help you to meet the following National Occupational Standards.
Key Role 1: Prepare for and work with individuals, families, carers, groups and communities to assess their needs and circumstances.
- Assess needs and options to recommend a course of action.

Key Role 2: Plan, carry out, review and evaluate social work practice, with individuals, families, carers, groups and communities and other professionals.
- Prepare, produce, implement and evaluate plans with individuals, families, carers, groups, communities and professional colleagues.

Key Role 4: Manage risk to individuals, families, carers, groups, communities, self and colleagues.
- Assess and manage risks to individuals, families, carers, groups and communities.
- Assess, minimise and manage risk to self and colleagues.

Key Role 5: Manage and be accountable, with supervision and support, for your own social work practice within your organisation.
- Manage, present and share records and reports.

Key Role 6: Demonstrate professional competence in social work practice.
- Research, analyse, evaluate and use current knowledge of best social work practice.

It will also introduce you to the following academic standards as set out in the social work subject benchmark statement.

3.1.4. Social work theory: models and methods of assessment – selection, professional judgement, processes of risk assessment.

3.1.5. Nature of social work practice: place of theoretical perspectives and evidence from international research on assessment and decision-making processes in social work.

3.2.2. Problem-solving skills:
- developing communication and information gathering skills in a range of ways, such as electronically, face-to-face and from others;
- assessing the reliability of information in complex situations;
- developing assessment and analysis skills that cut across intellectual and practical activities:
  - to choose the right model and approach
  - to practise in a way that takes different points of view into account
  - to evaluate ethical issues and the impact of discrimination.

Introduction

It has long been acknowledged that assessment is a key task in social work practice (Milner and O'Byrne, 2002; Bartlett, 1970). As beginning social workers you will be asked to complete, contribute to and present assessments during your practice learning for the degree and once qualified. It is important that you have a thorough knowledge of what makes a good assessment, how they are conducted and some of the difficulties that might arise when making an assessment. The centrality of good social work assessment is emphasised by the inquiry into the death of Victoria Climbié (Laming, 2003).

The inquiry puts centre stage some of the actions and responsibilities social workers need to take into account when making an assessment. For instance, when a referral is made concerning children they must be seen within 24 hours or the reasons why this cannot be achieved must be clearly recorded (recommendation 35). Where there are allegations of deliberate harm the social worker must:

- speak alone to the child;

- see and speak with carers;

- visit the child's accommodation;

- seek and consider the views of other professionals;

- agree a plan to provide for the child's welfare (recommendation 40).

In making these assessments, social workers should have the confidence to question other agencies and their involvement or conclusions (recommendation 37). This is not always easy and developing confidence demands that we as social workers know what it is we do and why we are doing it. This, again, is something that the Climbié inquiry focuses on. For instance, recommendation 34 states that social workers should not undertake home visits without being clear about the purpose of the visit, what information is being sought and what will happen if there is no one at home. It is also important that social workers check any prior information they have, if at all possible, and pay strict attention to recording visits and information gained on a case file. It is recognised that these responsibilities are demanding and the Climbié inquiry again states that social workers should receive regular supervision that considers case recording (recommendation 45).

Social workers undertake a wide range of assessments that are not solely confined to children in need and child protection including the following:

- community care assessments (s.47 National Health Service and Community Care Act 1990);

- specific assessment for carers (Carers [Recognition and Services] Act 1995);

- mental health assessments for admission to hospital or guardianship (Mental Health Act 1983, ss.2, 3, 4, 7).

In this chapter, you will be introduced to some definitions of assessment, types of assessment and key influences affecting social work assessments such as ethics, power, professionalism and anti-oppressive practice. You will be invited to consider how an assessment is made with service user groups common to social work – in child and family work and work with adults. As mentioned in the introduction, we will not cover all groups of people who use social services but cover a selection to illustrate key points. Contemporary guidance and advice on assessment in child care and in the single assessment process for older people will be provided and activities will help you to make links between knowledge and practice throughout this chapter. To illustrate some of the processes involved we will introduce our developing case studies later in the chapter. The importance of a multidisciplinary focus in assessments will be emphasised in terms of sharing information with other professionals, and from the perspective of service users who are unlikely to want to be assessed again and again for the same service by a number of agencies and professions (see Quinney, 2006). You will be asked to question the purpose and use of assessments, how they can be person-focused and proactive in achieving agreed aims. This will provide you with knowledge that you can use when considering the five key tools for use in assessment that will be introduced in Chapter 2.

The centrality of assessment work is recognised in social work education. Indeed, being skilled in conducting assessments is a key requirement for social workers and is recognised in the government's drive to improve social work education. It is reflected in the Teaching, Learning and Assessment Requirements for the qualifying degree:

> *...providers will have to demonstrate that all students undertake specific learning and assessment in the following key areas*
> * *assessment, planning, intervention and review.*
> (Department of Health, 2002a, pages 3–4)

So, learning about assessment, how to assess and developing skilled competence in making assessments is central to your development as a social worker. Before you can begin learning these skills, however, it is important to have some idea of what an assessment is and how one might be defined.

What is assessment? Definitional perspectives

This section introduces ways in which assessment might be understood. It is important to have an awareness of different understandings of assessment because the ways in which it is understood can affect what is done, how the assessment takes place, how information is used and interpreted and what plans are made as a result. This will affect the ways in which you work but also how service users, carers and other professionals involved in the assessment perceive the process and work with you.

It is often useful to start with a dictionary definition. The *Oxford English Dictionary* sees assessment in terms of judging or valuing the worth of something. This is an indication of a skilled activity by someone who is competent to judge between things of different value. It implies the use of standards against which something can be appraised. This certainly appears to be the case in many social work assessments. However, it leaves out the interactive and human context which also feature in social work assessments. The definition suggests that there are right and wrong situations or good and bad values; a suggestion that, in social work, demands critical appraisal.

Assessment: art or science?

The perceived conflict between social work as 'art' or as 'science' is central to the debate about definitions. The debate is well rehearsed in the literature (see Richmond, 1917; England, 1986; Reamer, 1993; Munro, 1998), and links to contemporary discussions concerning evidence-based practice (Webb, 2001, 2006). If assessment is an art it cannot be limited by definitions, structured questionnaires, checklists or even fully described, rather it would rely on the wisdom and skill of the assessor as refined through experience. This may leave people open to the whims of individual social workers and their particular views and beliefs. It would not provide a systematic approach or one that service users could expect to receive regardless of practitioner, team or region. If, on the other hand, it is a science, then assessments should be open to precise measurement and be practised effectively by following steps outlined in a 'technical manual' of social work. This could be seen as reducing human situations to a common standard and would not allow for diversity in setting, culture and interpretation of situations. Consider the following example:

CASE STUDY

John has contacted the local community mental health team. For some time he has felt depressed, lethargic and unable to cope with his job. The team leader has asked that an assessment be undertaken.

a. *Tim, a social worker from an arts-based approach, talks with John about his situation in a free-flowing and broad way. He decides on the basis of his assessment and his prior experience that John is particularly vulnerable and would benefit from intensive support from the team.*

b. *Janice takes a systematic and 'scientific' approach to assessment. Her assessment of John takes into account a range of risk and vulnerability indices that are validated by their use on groups of similar people. Her assessment scores John below the threshold of risk that would guarantee him eligibility to a service from the team.*

A balanced approach would suggest that social work assessment is both an art and a science since it involves wisdom, skills, appreciation of diversity and systematically applied knowledge in practice (Parker, 2007a). Clifford (1998) puts this well in describing the interconnected elements in assessment:

> *...assessment has to partake of scientific, theoretical, artistic, ethical and practical elements – something which has long been recognised by practitioners, and regarded as traditional in social work and all the helping professions.*
> (Clifford, 1998, page 233)

Let us return to the case of John.

CASE STUDY

A third social worker, Jeannette, would use her prior experience of social work with people in John's position, weighing that knowledge against the eligibility criteria of the agency and the structured assessment tools that are designed to assist decision-making. The difference between Jeannette and Janice is that Jeannette would see the assessment instruments as 'tools' for a job and not prescriptions.

The approach taken by Jeannette is echoed by Middleton (1997) who describes assessment in terms of its practical application although she does consider it to be an art. For her, assessment is:

> *the analytical process by which decisions are made. In a social welfare context, it is a basis for planning what needs to be done to maintain or improve a person's situation...Assessment involves gathering and interpreting information in order to understand a person and their circumstances; the desirability and feasibility of change and the services and resources which are necessary to effect it. It involves making judgements based on information.*
> (Middleton, 1997, page 5)

Values, diversity and service user involvement

Middleton (1997) locates the process of assessment firmly in the context of social work values and states that respect for individual differences is central if the process is not going to disempower the individual but enhance their strengths and coping abilities. The emphasis on values is important because assessments are about making judgements but not about being judgemental. Milner and O'Byrne (2002) identify several potential pitfalls in making judgements that we need to avoid. These include paying attention selectively, stereotyping and labelling people, attributing certain characteristics to people because we think that is how they are likely to behave and sensory distortions. Groups, agencies and teams, as well as individuals, can also be affected by developing collective assumptions and perspectives on situations; see the following case example.

CASE STUDY

Chris was well known in the social work office. Since having his first child removed from his care and subsequently freed and placed for adoption, he has been to the office on several occasions, becoming angry and shouting and swearing at the social work staff. Once he threatened violence to the social worker involved in the initial assessment.

Three years after this incident he has again come into contact with the social work team as he has become involved in a relationship with a woman who has two young children. Jeremy, a social worker new to the team, has been asked to assess the new situation. His colleagues have warned him about Chris's 'dangerousness'. Chris is a big man, sporting several tattoos on each arm and a 'skinhead' haircut. On first meeting Chris, Jeremy was quite nervous, and a little on edge when Chris became loud. Jeremy realised that Chris was wearing a hearing aid, and was being open and detailed about the past and present situation. He appeared to want to engage with him.

Starting from strengths, respect for service users and keeping clear records can assist in offsetting some of these difficulties. Milner and O'Byrne (2002) present a model of assessment that acknowledges that knowledge is developed through interactions with other people and does not necessarily proceed in a straight line between point A and point B.

> *We do not suggest that there is a single correct way to analyse human situations but encourage social workers to be reflexive and develop a pragmatic truth that fits social work situations in a way which is most satisfying for service users, the end product being a story that is **helpful** to all concerned.*
> (Milner and O'Byrne, 2002, page 4, emphasis in original)

This is important if we are going to avoid labelling people like Chris in the case study above, and if we are to undertake comprehensive and valid assessments.

The reduction of individual situations to a set of problems and causes may suggest that there are clear 'right and wrong' actions and situations that can be observed and assessed. The constraint of resources and the setting of eligibility criteria to restrict access to services compound this view according to Milner and O'Byrne. Assessments are rarely, if ever, 'value-free' and the particular perspectives of social workers influence the way they are conducted and their analysis (see Rees, 1991). It is imperative, therefore, that workers should be aware of and check their individual bias and how this may well affect the assessment undertaken (Clifford, 1998).

Milner and O'Byrne (2002) suggest social workers acknowledge the power they have in making assessments and that multiple interpretations of situations are considered. Negotiation between service users and social workers and the construction of a joint narrative form the basis of their assessment approach. Assessment concerns the development of a social narrative that takes into account diversity. Writing from a child care perspective, Cooper (2000) argues that when social workers are reflexive – identifying, questioning their own biases and ensuring assessments are interactive and collaborative – it is possible to create effective interpersonal relationships and offset potential bias. Social workers need, in their assessments, to listen to people, validate their experiences and work collaboratively to promote service users' strengths. This is something with which Fook (2002) also agrees. She considers the traditional and accepted approach to assessment involves sorting into categories and creating eligible and ineligible types. The common element being to frame situations in terms of 'problems' which fit those holding the power and resources. The alternative approach allows for multiple and diverse understandings developed in the particular context of the individuals involved. The models developed by Milner and O'Byrne and Fook use a narrative approach that is constructed with the service user and is open to change and development. Assessment becomes a process of dialogue rather than fact-finding. It is also important not to be bound to restrictive assessment proformas but to question what information is needed, why it is needed and to what uses it might be put. Let us return briefly to the case study of Chris.

CASE STUDY

In developing a working relationship with Chris, Jeremy was able to allow him time to rehearse his past experiences with social workers, the hurt he had felt and the anger that it had aroused in him. Jeremy was also able to put forward the reasons why the actions had been taken and the responsibilities that social workers have. Whilst this was painful for Chris, it allowed him to work with Jeremy in a more open and collaborative way. They were able to discuss together ways in which progress might be made.

Theory and assessment

One problem in defining and understanding assessment is that there have been very few attempts to construct a systematic theory of assessment in social work (Lloyd and Taylor, 1995). Coulshed and Orme (2006) describe how assessment may be understood by its core processes, its purposes or its theoretical base. What is clear is that the theoretical approach taken by social workers and the agencies in which they work influences the assessment process in a similar way to personal values and beliefs systems. Social workers need to acknowledge not only their personal beliefs, values and biases but also the impact their approaches might have on the way an assessment proceeds. Social workers should be open, honest and explicit with service users (Coulshed and Orme, 2006). For instance, Howe (1992) identifies a range of broad theoretical categories that can be adopted in social work that take either:

- a problem-solving perspective, starting from the position that there is something wrong that needs to be fixed, whether in the present (cognitive-behavioural), or in the past (psychoanalytic);

- a perspective that is concerned with the construction of subjective experiences or how people understand their experiences within society, how labels are applied to people on the basis of their actions;

- a political model that considers social problems in relation to social inequalities and the dominant political system.

Each of these approaches to social work affects the way an assessment proceeds. Consider the following case study and the different responses that might be made depending on the perspective or approach of the social worker.

CASE STUDY

Jane, mother of Tony, separated from Eddie, Tony's father, after two years of domestic violence. Tony received an injury to his arm during one of these incidents. Eddie is now requesting greater contact with Tony.

A social worker taking a problem-solving approach would look to examine the risks that Eddie might pose to Tony and seek and test alternatives or ways of reducing any risks. This social worker might assess the capacities for change, development and protection of those involved.

A social worker from the second school of thought might assess the impact the situation might have on Tony, whether or not he wished for contact and the meanings that a lack of contact might have for both Tony and Eddie, and indeed Jane. This social worker might also explore how being seen as violent might impact on Eddie's capacity for change.

A social worker taking a more overt political approach may look to the problems that male domination has led to in creating a context in which violence towards women is seen as acceptable and where women are seen as victims. This social worker may also take a class-based analysis looking at education, employment and environmental factors that may have contributed to the previous situation.

Social work assessments, therefore, combine the judgement or weighing up of something with the explicit acknowledgement of the importance of values, diversity and the views of others. One further way of looking at assessment in social work is to separate the 'types' of assessment used.

Assessment types in social work

In this section, we will examine the different types of assessment in terms of their focus and duration. Before we look at different types of assessment it is important to take a little time to consider the question, 'Why is assessment so important?' We have seen the stress put on assessment in the Climbié inquiry. It is, however, not a discrete entity that can be undertaken in isolation from other aspects of social work and social care practice. Assessment is an integral part of the social work process and, certainly in practice, assessment and intervention cannot be clearly separated. Assessment is part of a continual process which links with planning, intervening and reviewing social work with service users. This is exemplified well in the ASPIRE model:

AS – Assessment

P – Planning

I – Intervention

RE – Review and Evaluation
(Sutton, 1999)

If assessment is effective then it makes it more likely that intervention will succeed (Milner and O'Byrne, 2002). Assessment is the key to effective social work practice in whichever area you are working and also a central task in contemporary social work (McDonald, 2006). Watson and West (2006, page 30) state:

Assessment is at the heart of all good social work practice. It covers a spectrum of activities, from observation and judgements made within the context of an initial encounter through to more formal and complex frameworks of assessment. Its purpose is to enhance understanding of the service user's situation, helping workers to identify areas for potential change that will assist the development of a rationale for future intervention.

Unfortunately, when assessments are undertaken the converse is also true. When assessments are undertaken without adequate preparation and without a clear sense of purpose and direction they are unlikely to produce good quality material that will help in planning to improve the lot of service users. The following case study illustrates some reasons for paying attention to planning for assessment and specifying purpose.

CASE STUDY

As a student on her first practice learning placement, Margaret was allocated a case concerning a mother, Carol, and her two young children. The referral from the health visitor had requested help with parenting and behaviour management.

Margaret was eager to begin practice. She telephoned Carol and organised a convenient time and date to visit. The day of the visit arrived. Margaret made her way to the house, rang the bell and introduced herself when Carol answered. It was at this point that she realised she had no plan, did not know what information to collect, how to collect it and to what ends she was making an assessment. Carol asked Margaret what she was going to do to help her with her children. Margaret did not know how to answer. The visit became tense and after 15 minutes ended with no further plans. Carol telephoned her health visitor the following day to say the social worker was 'useless'.

Fortunately, you are not likely to be placed in such a position because you will have a practice assessor who will help you to plan and prepare for visits. However, this case example illustrates some of the difficulties that can arise when planning is inadequate or when the social worker has not clarified their role and the reasons for and expected outcomes of the assessment visit.

In social work, assessments can be separated into two basic types – ongoing and fluid, or time-limited and issues specific. Superficially, these two types may be seen as corresponding to the debate about social work as an art or as a science. In practice, these two types are more complex and often assessments comprise elements of both. Coulshed and Orme (2006) are clear, for instance, that assessment does not simply represent a singular event, but continues after the production of a specific piece of work or report.

Assessment as an ongoing, fluid and dynamic process

Assessment is increasingly acknowledged to be a continuous process (Hepworth, Rooney and Larsen, 1997; Coulshed and Orme, 2006; Department of Health, Department for Education and Employment, Home Office, 2000). This develops the *what* and *how* that need to be done but acknowledges that changes and developments occur in a person's life that may have a significant impact on how a situation is seen or responded to. It is something that continues over time. The benefits of this approach lie in seeing social work as a process in which assessment and intervention are interconnected and that social work is a dynamic activity that changes throughout its course (see Chapter 4). It also clearly associates assessment and evaluation in the social work process. Pincus and Minahan (1973) develop this 'process' model of assessment in their systemic approach to social work practice:

> *The process of assessment...continues throughout the planned change process while the initial assessment serves as a blueprint it will be modified as ideas are tested out and new data and information are gathered. The worker continually reassesses the nature of the problem, the need for supporting data and the effectiveness of the approaches chosen to cope with it.*
> *(Pincus and Minahan, 1973, page 116)*

Single event/time-specific formulations

In practice, however, social workers sometimes do not continue the assessment throughout a planned piece of work (Clifford, 1998). In fact, community care law and practice may preclude such a continuous process because of the separation of assessment as a discrete activity (McDonald, 2006) and the development of a split between assessing and commissioning or purchasing functions and the provision of services.

A second way of categorising assessment in social work is as a *time-specific formulation* (Hepworth, Rooney and Larsen, 1997). This means the production of a report after a time-limited period of assessment has taken place. For instance, a court report, a report for a case conference or an initial community care assessment report may represent such a type of assessment.

It is this kind of assessment that may suggest there are clear norms and standards. The assessment judges aspects of the service user's life against expected or accepted ways of seeing similar situations. It offers a way of examining a situation, event or individual within a specific timescale or period in a person's life. This focused approach lends itself to making predictions or identifying needs, goals and ways of achieving these. It also offers, at times, a baseline, from which change can be continually monitored. It does not, however, necessarily tell you anything about the individuals or events except at this particular point in time. It may not present a full or accurate picture that holds over time or in different circumstances and it may reflect the values of those making the assessment rather than those being assessed. This is where the development of practice wisdom becomes important.

The debate is extended by the increasing recognition that spirituality forms an important part of comprehensive assessments that focus on potential service user strengths (Hodge, 2001; Gotterer, 2001). This links with the attitudes and beliefs of social workers who need to acknowledge their own belief systems whilst respecting those of others. Often spirituality can be confused with religion and, again, social workers need to take care in making assumptions that can skew assessments.

ACTIVITY *1.1*

Write down as many reasons as you can think of for social workers undertaking an assessment. Place these in three lists:

- *those that focus on producing reports or specific products;*
- *those that see assessment as a continuous process;*
- *those that fall into both categories.*

Comment

The activity above may not have been as easy as it may have seemed at first sight. Indeed, you may have hesitated when placing each assessment in one of the three columns. Don't worry if this was the case. Assessments are, as we are beginning to see, complex and do not fit neatly into categories. Even an assessment that resulted in a court report, or case conference report, might be seen as a stepping stone to further assessment work, and an open assessment may have produced a summary and 'measuring point' from which progress or changes can be determined.

Risk assessment

The concept of risk has assumed increasing importance within our daily lives and activites (Webb, 2006). This is also the case in respect of social work practice and assessment. Risk can be understood in actuarial terms as the likelihood of certain outcomes, whether positive or negative, occuring under certain circumstances or dependent on decisions made. Whether or not it is believed that such calculations can be made accurately in social work, the regulations of risk has become central to contemporary practice. Webb sees the assessment of risk as a problem in social work, suggesting that:

> *Its methods are based on strong notions of predictability and calculation that a future event is likely to occur... These partly rely on exisitng scientific knowledge, which is often provided by experts. In social work the assessment of risk often lacks scientific rigour and may not be modelled in a satisfactory way... Risk assessment is pervaded by value-laden assumptions and is often used as a rationing device that excludes some from service provision.* (Webb, 2006, page 19)

However, it is important to mention risk assesment here as you will be required to complete such assessments in your work and understanding some of the complicating factors, as pointed out above, can be helpful. The assessment of risk is uncertain and accurate predictions not always possible but it can provide a framework for honest discussions which allows those using services to make informed choices (Watson and West, 2006). Coulshed and Orme (2006) promote Corby's earlier work on risk assessment in child protection identifying three elements of risk assessment, and suggest this can be adapted for different settings. The three elements are associated with the stage in the process at which they are undertaken (see box 1.)

> ### Box 1: Types of Risk Assessment, after Coulshed and Orme (2006)
> **Types of Risk Assessment**
>
> | | *Preventive risk assessment* | *Investigative risk assessment* | *Continuation risk assessment* |
> |---|---|---|---|
> | *Process stage* | prior to intervention | intial contact and assessment stage | continuing involvement |
> | *Key questions* | Should anything be done? | What is happening here? | Has the risk reduced? |
> | *Comment* | relies on research evidence which is often equivocal | procedures, guidelines and checklists may be interpreted too prescriptively | balances risks of intervening against not intervening |

All these forms of risk assessment have their own inherent 'risks' and it is important to remember that an individualised, reflective approach needs to be maintained when conducting such assessments.

Levels of assessment in social work

As well as looking at assessment by type, we can also distinguish between the levels of assessment. By this we mean whether the assessment is broad-based, fluid and holistic (taking into account all aspects of the service user's life and situation), or whether it is focused on a particular issue or serves to inform a particular intervention. These levels do not necessarily preclude one another. It may be appropriate in many circumstances to undertake a broad social assessment prior to focusing on an agreed goal and target for intervention which may demand a much more specific focus and activity. In practice, social work assessments often reflect not only different levels throughout the intervention but contain elements of both types identified in the previous section. Doel and Marsh (1992) use a helpful illustration to show the importance of levels in an assessment for task-centred social work. They employ the example of a newspaper which can be scanned by its headlines to give an indication of what topics are covered. If there are articles of particular interest you might read the first paragraph or indeed the whole article depending on your focus at the time. Another way of considering the refinement of an assessment is to think of a funnel tapering towards the bottom. As you 'pour in' your information it will gradually be refined until the key elements remain. An example of this funnel approach is shown below.

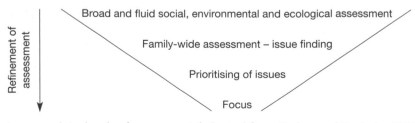

A funnel approach to levels of assessment (adapted from Parker and Penhale, 1998)

Being explicit about the type used and the implications of this for service users is important. The type and level of assessment used will have implications for the service received and the approach employed. If service users are to be fully involved in the assessment, an understanding of what will take place, how it will proceed and for what reasons the information is being gathered is crucial. The example below presents a way of conceptualising social work assessments by type and level.

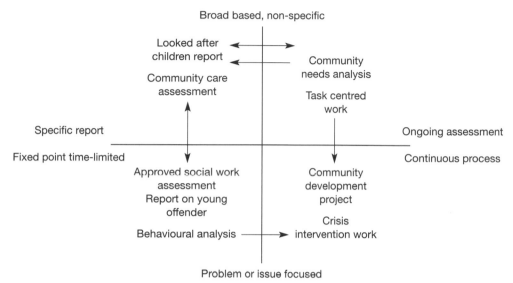

Assessment types and levels (with some examples)

The issues or interventions given as examples in the diagram above change and shift between points on the matrix. However, it provides a helpful visual way of identifying some of the key features of an assessment.

The purpose of assessment in social work

The purposes of assessment are as many and varied as the methods designed for undertaking them. The assessment itself serves to reach initial conclusions that describe, explain, predict, evaluate and prescribe or suggest interventive methods. Thus it has a purposive element and to achieve its purpose assessment should be focused, factual and explicit. Assessments have often followed resource-led pathways (those dependent on what services are available at the time) rather than the broader needs-led approach (looking not at what is available but what is needed to make a difference) which is now in vogue. The needs-led approach separates out ends and means and is not dependent upon the resources available. It is hoped that by taking this view the larger picture will help clarify and identify service gaps and therefore allow for ways of filling these. However, Coulshed and Orme (2006) relate this to the 'real world' and state that needs-led principles cannot work unless there are plenty of resources and that in social work there will always be a situation where demand exceeds supply and a judgement must be made between competing needs.

For writers who consider social work as a purposeful activity, there has long been an association between assessment and a problem solving approach to working with service users.

> *The problem solving model...demands that the client's purposes and expectations in joining the worker in interaction be explored and understood and kept in the centre of concern. It is our firm conviction that lack of initial exploration of expectations and goals and lack of careful selection of the starting place in the contact phase...account for a large percentage of the failures in the helping process.*
> (Compton and Galloway, 1975, page 285)

This is now reflected within the National Occupational Standards and the subject benchmark criteria for social work. In essence, we can state that a social work assessment is a focused collation, analysis and synthesis of relevant collected data pertaining to the presenting problem and identified needs. They are often confused with evaluation but are, in fact, *more akin to an exploratory study which forms the basis for decision-making and action* (Coulshed and Orme, 2006, page 26). This problem-solving model may suggest that a focused and scientific approach is being advocated. However, it must be remembered that the model is intended to be collaborative and works effectively if service users work together with the social worker in an active exploration of the issues. Perhaps this purposeful approach would benefit from being balanced with a strengths-based model which takes into account the capacities and resources of the service user.

Strengths and social exclusion

Hepworth, Rooney and Larsen (1997) stress the importance of including service users' strengths in assessments. Past social work practices focused upon pathology and appeared to ignore strengths for change. This created dependency and was seen as damaging to a service user's self-esteem. An individual's needs do not occur in isolation, however. Problems are often complex, involve other people and agencies and occur in a variety of social situations. Therefore, an assessment requires extensive knowledge of the service user's environmental and living system and the wider systems impinging upon it.

Working with service user strengths helps ensure that an anti-oppressive focus is maintained, that the values of social work are promoted and that individual and self-responsibility are emphasised. The strengths perspective focuses on positives with the intention of increasing motivation, capacity and potential for making real and informed life choices as Saleeby (1996) states.

> *The strengths perspective honors two things: the power of the self to heal and right itself with the help of the environment, and the need for an alliance with the hope that life might really be otherwise. Helpers must hear the individual, family, or community stories, but people can write the story of their near and far failures only if they know everything they need to know about their condition and circumstances. The job is to help individuals and groups develop the language, summon the resources, devise the plot, and manage the subjectivity of life in their world.*
> (Saleeby, 1996, page 303)

Pierson (2002) understands the assessment of children in need as being similar to the central concept of social exclusion in social work. Both draw attention to the wider environment and ecological factors (those relating to the individual's living situation) in the lives of children, young people and families, and the structural barriers people face. Where he differs is in promoting the strengths-based approach as opposed to a deficit model. The strengths perspective focuses on resilience, survival in the face of significant hardship or threat to well-being. There is room within the assessment framework to focus on the cognitive skills, coping mechanisms, temperamental and dispositional factors, interpersonal skills and social supports that can be built on as strengths. He uses Saleeby's model to examine barriers and strengths shown in the following diagram.

Saleeby's strengths and barriers model (see Pierson, 2002)

Taking a strengths-based or solution focused approach demands a change in emphasis for social workers. No longer can they be seen as expert but as collaborators, facilitating service users to identify their needs and explore alternative ways of acting or conceptualising their experiences. This can be achieved by adopting Smale, Tuson and Statham's (2000) perspective on assessment in which social workers do not act as 'experts' questioning service users, or simply follow agency procedures. Rather, social workers develop an exchange model similar to Fook's (2002) notion of the joint construction of a narrative. The exchange model acknowledges that service users are the experts on their situations. It sees service users and social workers exchanging ideas, information and ways forward to make a difference and find alternative ways of approaching the situation being considered.

A strengths-based approach aims to reduce some of the imbalance in power between social workers and service users. It must be acknowledged, however, that the power will never be fully balanced and there are times when social workers are empowered by law to undertake assessments. It is central in these cases for social workers to be honest and open with service users as indicated by Parker (2007a, page 116):

> *While social workers necessarily employ procedures, they can still use an exchange model in their work. Indeed, the spirit underlying many procedures demands that social workers advance collaborative exchanges that put users centre stage.*

Skills in assessment

Watson and West (2006) suggest that effective assessment depends on the deployment of key skills especially communication, negotiation and decision-making. Whilst these interpersonal skills are certainly important, it must be remembered that administrative skills are also central to accurate and purposeful assessment (see Coulshed and Orme, 2006).

Assessment demands an ability to *organise, systematise and rationalise* knowledge gathered. Concurrently, the social work has to be sensitive and demonstrate an ability to be able to value *the uniqueness of each individual* assessed.

As well as administrative, communication and written skills in undertaking assessments social workers need to develop and use listening and hearing skills when working with children, observing them and especially in engaging with and talking to them. This may involve using a range of activities to facilitate communication. In research that the Department of Health, Department for Education and Employment, Home Office (2000) cites, children prefer:

- to be listened to;

- professionals to be available and accessible;

- professionals to be non-judgemental and non-directive;

- professionals to have a sense of humour;

- straight talking;

- to be able to trust professionals and, where appropriate, to have confidentiality respected.

It is, of course, not always possible for information to be kept confidential. Social workers must inform service users of the times at which information cannot be kept confidential and will need to be shared with others. This should be done at the outset to the assessment process and not left until the matter arises in the course of an assessment.

ACTIVITY **1.2**

List the administrative and interpersonal skills that you think are needed to conduct an effective assessment. Identify which skills you already have, which you need to develop and outline ways in which you may increase these skills. Refer back to the standards and benchmarks detailed at the outset of this chapter and match these against your answers.

You may have included your ability to write clearly, to organise a system to store and file information. Or perhaps you have considered the importance you attach to matters of confidentiality ensuring that privacy procedures are carried out to the letter. Some of the interpersonal skills you might have identified concern communication in written reports and letters, face-to-face or on the telephone, and indeed use of information and communication technologies. Try to think of the skills that you have not added to your list and think of how you might develop these in your practice.

Hepworth, Rooney and Larsen (1997) emphasise that assessment is critical to social work intervention and its effectiveness. This leads to the identification of goals for change, means for achieving these and alternatives. Since assessments can be construed as fluid and dynamic the assessment changes as the change process proceeds. Bartlett (1970) states that it is only after understanding and identifying relevant factors in any situation that plans to act may be formulated (Coulshed and Orme, 2006; Parker, 2007a). Thus, we can say that the purpose of assessment in social work is to acquire and study information about people in their environment to decide upon an identified problem and to plan effective options to resolve that problem. It must also be remembered that assessments are not simply fact-finding exercises but represent a joint construction of a narrative or story between social workers and service users. Remembering this helps to locate the assessment in context and draws attention to issues of power when undertaking assessment work.

Characteristics and features of assessments

Most writers agree on the features comprising an assessment although models differ slightly as shown in Table 1.1. Also the ways in which different teams collect and organise their information will differ depending on the purpose of the assessment, the focus of the team and the particular approaches taken. It is generally helpful, however, to have a framework in mind when gathering information. This can help you to engage with service users who will want to know what information you want to collect and why you might want to do so. Having a clear understanding of what you are doing and why can also help you create an atmosphere that is more participative and negotiated.

Table 1.1 Characteristics of assessments

	Cournoyer (1991)	Hepworth, Rooney and Larsen (1997)	Middleton (1997)	Milner and O'Byrne (2002)
Preparation, planning and engagement		**Clarification of ecological factors** including a configuration of the systems involved.	Establishing a working relationship Timing Ground rules Acknowledging feelings	**Preparation** Identify key people Create a schedule for data collection Determine the interview schedule Produce a statement of intent and include purpose and systems of accountability Note tentative explanations
Data collection and creating a problem profile	**Description** A. Client identification information B. Description of person system, family/household/ primary social system, and ecological system C. Presenting problems and goals D. Strengths and resources	**Identification of the problem**. This should be person centred although, of course, this is recognised to be difficult in the case of involuntary users of social work services. (This comes first in Hepworth and Larsen's model) Rooney	Data collection Individual wants Barriers, problems, stresses, resources and supports Coping mechanisms Evidence from professional/expert sources	**Data collection** Create a contents page for the case file Store data Check verbal data by summarising and reporting Check written data and mark opinion clearly Consider other sources of information

Table 1.1 Characteristics of assessments (continued)

	Cournoyer (1991)	Hepworth, Rooney and Larsen (1997)	Middleton (1997)	Milner and O'Byrne (2002)
	E. Referral source and process; collateral information F. Social history			Note inconsistencies but keep an open mind
Preliminary analysis of data	Tentative assessment A. Person B. Family/household/ primary social systems C. Ecology/environment D. Summary assessment	**Assessment of developmental wants and needs.** Stresses associated with life transitions.		**Weighing the data** Consider seriousness of situation or how well service user is functioning Identify persistent themes or patterns and list them Cluster themes and begin to rank in order of importance Identify gaps Identify people to help Develop a reflexive approach List people to be consulted
Testing the data, deep analysis		**Assessment of developmental wants and needs** Stresses associated with life transitions.	Analysis Individual wants Changes required Risks Opportunities Roles Costs Alternatives and options	**Analysing the data** Identify and using theories to gain a depth of analysis Develop hypotheses around goals Develop tentative explanations Test explanations for theoretical fit Check with key people involved Check data again Consult with reflexive group Develop further explanations and list ways they can be tested
Use of data, creating an action plan	Contract A. Problems B. Final goals C. Plans		Planning Draft proposals Negotiation Recommendations Reviews Quality assurance	**Utilising the data** What help is needed and by whom? List outcomes to be achieved and consequences to avoid Explain how outcomes can be measured Prepare intervention plan Develop independent mechanism to monitor outcomes – supervision, service user, multi-agency group Prepare draft report listing sources of information, analysis, initial judgement Obtain feedback on report and revise it accordingly

Specific uses of assessment with children and families and in care management

We will now consider how your developing knowledge of assessment applies to two key areas of social work practice. We will look first at assessments in social work with children and families, considering recent Department of Health guidance and the Climbié inquiry. We will follow this by looking at changing assessment practice in care management – social work with adults – and in particular with older people. To illustrate how an assessment might be undertaken we will introduce case study material in each situation. These case studies will develop throughout the rest of the book.

Framework for assessment of children in need and their families

The *Framework for assessment of children in need and their families* (Department of Health, Department for Education and Employment, Home Office, 2000, page viii) *provides a systematic way of analysing, understanding and recording what is happening to children and young people within their families and the wider context of the community in which they live*. If you are planning to work in child care you will need a thorough understanding of the *Framework*. Whereas assessment in the Children Act 2004 relates to inspection, review or investigation of children's services – a type of assessment we will not cover here – the *Framework* builds on the duties of assessment of needs set out in section 17 and Schedule 2 para 3 of the Children Act 1989:

> *Where it appears to a local authority that a child within their area is in need, the authority may assess his needs for the purposes of this Act...*

It also builds on responsibilities under section 47 of the Children Act which obliges local authorities to consider making inquiries if concerns have been expressed about a child's well-being or possible maltreatment. An assessment in this case would be made to determine whether a child was suffering or likely to suffer significant harm. Social workers carry a great deal of responsibility for this process and it is important that the assessment is comprehensive and effective. However, it must be remembered that assessments under section 47 involve a shared responsibility and any plans or action taken will be in consultation with supervisors, managers and with other professionals.

The *Framework* stresses the need for interagency co-operation and maintaining clarity about the following areas:

- the purpose of the assessment and anticipated outputs;
- the legislative basis for the assessment;
- the protocols and procedures used;
- which agency, team and professional has lead responsibility;
- how the child and family members will be involved;
- which professional has the lead responsibility for analysing the assessment findings and developing a plan;
- the respective roles of the professionals involved;

- the ways in which the information will be shared;
- the professional responsible for taking the plan forward.

The principles on which the assessment are based consist of:

- being child-centred;
- being informed by child development theories;
- being ecological in approach;
- ensuring equality of opportunity;
- involving children and families in the process;
- building on strengths as well as identifying difficulties;
- an interagency approach;
- seeing assessment as a continuous process and not a single event;
- assessments being carried out in tandem with other actions and services;
- being grounded in evidence-based knowledge.

The *Framework* provides a systematic approach that can be individually tailored. In this way it seeks to be both an art and a science that can apply threshold criteria of need to each individual taking into account diverse circumstances and situations. Each assessment covers three key areas relating to the development of the child, the capacities of parents and caregivers to respond to needs and the impact of wider family and environmental factors (see diagram below). These three domains interact and the analysis of the child's needs is used to develop a clear plan of action to secure the best outcomes for the child. A range of useful tools and methods for undertaking assessments using the *Framework* are detailed by Fowler (2003), and a useful introduction is provided by Horwath (2001).

The following diagram shows the 'assessment triangle'.

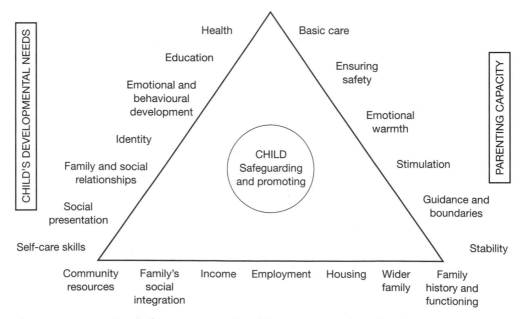

The assessment triangle (Department of Health, Department for Education and Employment, Home Office, 2000)

The stress on systematic and evidence based assessment is clear. The social worker's role in conducting an assessment is to plan for the assessment and, in order to account for the complexity of the task should gather and record information in a systematic and precise way, checking information with the child and parents. Where there are differences over information these should be recorded and strengths and difficulties should be acknowledged. The assessment should be child-centred and therefore the impact of the situation on the child must be clearly identified (see Chapter 2).

The *Framework* follows a number of phases that each have clear timescales attached. The phases of the assessment concern clarifying the source of the referral and reason for it, the gathering of existing information, exploring facts and feelings, exploring differences between family, child and professional understandings and feelings, and drawing together an analysis of needs within the family and local community context. Timescales are tight and demand a high level of skill and good management of the process. A decision about the likely response should be made within one working day of receipt of a referral and an initial assessment should be completed within seven working days. If a core assessment is to be undertaken this should be completed within 35 working days of the referral being made. The core assessment is an important document for which the social worker has considerable responsibility. It may be used within family proceedings, as evidence in support of threshold criteria, issues relating to the welfare checklist and as a rationale for the care plan for the child. This demands, therefore, that assessments should be planned, undertaken in partnership with children and families and recorded appropriately.

The *Framework* also acknowledges that assessment is a continuous process and that individual factors make assessments very diverse:

> *The Guidance has emphasised that assessment is not an end in itself but a process which will lead to an improvement in the wellbeing or outcomes for a child or young person. The conclusion of an assessment should result in:*
>
> - *an analysis of the needs of the child and the parenting capacity to respond appropriately to those needs within their family context;*
>
> - *identification of whether and, if so, where intervention will be required to secure the wellbeing of the child or young person;*
>
> - *a realistic plan of action (including services to be provided), detailing who has a responsibility for action, a timetable and a process for review.*

(Department of Health, Department for Education and Employment, Home Office, 2000, 4.1, page 53)

The government's *Every Child Matters* agenda seeks to improve opportunities, outcomes and services for children and young people in five key areas:

- Being healthy

- Staying safe

- Enjoying and achieving

- Making a positive contribution

- Achieving economic well-being.

The thrust of this policy has led to the development of a Common Assessment Framework (CAF) to aid the assessment of children's needs. It represents a standardised approach designed to promote interagency cooperation but is not an approach for use in the investigation of suspected harm or risk of harm which would follow the agreed protocol of local safeguarding children boards. The CAF is being introduced gradually until the end of 2008 whithin children's services (interdisciplinary children's teams brought about by the Children Act 2004 and *National Service Framework* for Children (Department for Education and Skills/Department of Health, 2004). It is likely that you will be able to note some of the common ground between the *Framework* and the CAF.

The CAF aims to be a comprehensive tool that, with training, will help practitioners identify children's additional or complex needs and coordinates and complements rather than replaces specialist disciplinary assessments. The process is flexible but involves:

Preparation identifying the possibility of additional needs perhaps using the CAF checklist which can be found at **www.ecm.gov.uk/caf**

Discussion gathering information about strengths and needs involving the child and parents/carers. The CAF discussion has eight stages:

1. explaining the purpose of the assessment

2. identifying details about the child

3. assessment information – who was present at the assessment, consultation with others

4. details of parents and carers

5. current family and home situation

6. details of all services working with the child

7. main assessment areas covering child development, how well parents are able to support the child's development and respond appropriately to their needs and the family and environmental situation having an impact on the family. It is this section that builds on the *Framework* and you should familiarise yourself with it by consulting the documents at **www.ecm.gov.uk/caf**

8. conclusions, solutions and actions including what will be done, by whom and timescales and review

Delivery services and identified actions are brought in, undertaken and coordinated as appropriate.

The following case study introduces some of the issues that arise when using the assessment *Framework* or the CAF. This case study will develop throughout the book and it will be important to return to it at various stages in your reading to check how practice might develop with children and families.

CASE STUDY

Melissa is a single mother aged 16. She lives with her 9-month-old daughter, Rebecca, in a one-bedroomed flat owned by a local Housing Association. She has recently begun to spend an increasing amount of time with a young man Ian, whom she met several weeks ago. Ian seems to be very attentive to both Melissa and Rebecca. Melissa's mother Irene, herself in her early thirties, does not approve of Melissa seeing this man. She believes she should devote her time to Rebecca and mentions her own experiences as a young mother to back up this statement.

Melissa disagrees and she visits Ian and his father frequently for a number of weeks. It seems that Rebecca responds well to the introduction of another attentive person into her life. According to the health visitor, she is developing appropriately for her age and seems attentive and bright. However, she has been suffering from an increasing number of stomach bugs, and is not eating as well as she used to. In fact, Melissa has become a little concerned because Rebecca has lost weight consistently over the last two weeks. She has taken Rebecca to the doctor who suggested 'keeping an eye' on her.

A few days ago Melissa's mother visited when Melissa and her young man were in bed smoking marijuana. Irene was horrified, it being 2 o'clock in the afternoon, and reported them to the police and social services. She insisted that her granddaughter was in 'moral danger and should be taken away and adopted'. Melissa said Rebecca was asleep and asked what harm there was in what they were doing.

The first action the duty social worker made was to explore with Irene, Melissa's mother, the substance of her concerns, to gather basic information and to ascertain whether Melissa was aware of the referral. The social worker, Mandy, then recorded this information on the childcare referral form used by her agency. A copy of this is shown in the figure overleaf.

*The information gathered from Irene was checked with her as the form was being completed. Mandy explained that she would need to speak to her team leader before deciding the next step. She also informed Irene of the department's policy of supporting children and families to stay together. Mandy then took the completed form to her team leader, Geoff, to consider how to proceed. Geoff and Mandy checked existing records to see if anything was known about Melissa, Rebecca and family but there was no information found. Mandy and Geoff considered the information that had been given by Irene and agreed after beginning to complete a pre-assessment checklist (**www.ecm.gov.uk/caf**), as Irene had indicated, that the referral did not constitute an urgent case. However, they also agreed that it was important to make further enquiries, to see Melissa and Rebecca and to check the concerns regarding stomach ailments. Since an allegation of potential harm was made and the referral had also been made to the police, Mandy's team leader spoke with the contact Inspector, Lynne Davies, to agree the proposed course of action. Inspector Davies informed Geoff that they were taking no further action in respect of substance use and had advised Irene to contact social services. It was agreed that there was no need for a joint investigation between social workers and police officers at this time. This decision was documented clearly and attached to the form.*

Melissa had no telephone and Mandy did not know whether she had any difficulties reading letters. However, she decided to send a letter stating a time and date for a visit as a matter of courtesy but was prepared to explain the reason for the visit when she arrived.

CHILDCARE REFERRAL FORM 1 SOUTHSIDE SOCIAL SERVICES DEPARTMENT

Family Name: Krajic   Given Name: Rebecca

Also known as (AKA): N/A

Date of birth/Age: 9 months   Gender: F   Ethnicity: White British   Religion: Not specified

Address: Flat 10 Southfield   Recent address: 5 Northway Ave
          South Street   Southside
          Southside

Postcode: ST1 1HS   Postcode: ST3 2SW

Tel. No. N/A   Tel. No.   01111 234234

GP/Health Visitor: Dr Braye/   School: N/A
                 June Bridge

Members of Household

Family Name	Given Name	AKA	Gender	Ethnicity	Relationship	DOB	Parental responsibility
Krajic	Melissa	N/A	F	White Br	mother	16 years	Y

Significant Others

Krajic	Irene	N/A	F	White Br	G'mother	34 years	N

Professionals involved

Name	Profession	Contact details
June Bridge	Health Visitor	Dr Braye's surgery 01111 321321

Source of referral: Grandmother

Reason for Referral
Grandmother believes her nine month old granddaughter is at risk of neglect from her mother, Melissa. She is concerned that Melissa's boyfriend has no experience with children and poses a threat to Rebecca. G'mother thinks Rebecca should be adopted and has also passed on her concerns to the police who suggested contacting SSD.
The reasons for concern centre on Rebecca being left in her cot whilst Melissa and her boyfriend had sex in the adjoining room. She reports also an increase in the number of stomach complaints Rebecca seems to have.

Is client aware of referral?: Y

Receiving social worker: Mandy Jones
Date: 10.05.03

Child care referral form

Geoff and Mandy set to planning an initial assessment of Rebecca's situation and needs. This would include the following:

- *a visit to Melissa and Rebecca;*

- *discussion with Melissa, her boyfriend, and observation of living situation focusing on the three aspects of the assessment triangle;*

- *seeking an agreement to contact the health visitor;*

- *contacting the health visitor and discussing Rebecca's development and the reported stomach problems;*

- *discussing and explaining the limits of confidentiality and the need to share information between health visitor and social services;*

- *sharing an initial assessment fully with Melissa;*

- *agreeing, where possible, any further action that might be necessary.*

Melissa appeared happy to see Mandy when she visited. She said she had not seen the letter but was aware that a social worker would be coming as her mother had told her of her concerns. Melissa stated that she wanted the opportunity to put her case forward, stating that Irene had continued to 'interfere' in her care of Rebecca since she was born and that Irene feels guilty in Melissa's view because 'she was so crap at looking after me'.

The initial assessment covered information taken from the three areas outlined in stage 7 of the CAF and in the assessment triangle – developmental issues, parenting capacity, and family and environmental factors. Whilst these covered clear areas and the assessment could have been a simple 'question and answer' session, Mandy used her skills in forming relationships and communicating to develop her understanding of these areas. This was particularly important when discussing potentially sensitive areas such as parenting capacity and Melissa's own experiences of family life and functioning.

From the information that was discussed, Mandy began to form a picture of Melissa as a concerned young mother who was finding it difficult to care for Rebecca without some respite or support, especially when she was vomiting, ill or crying for long periods. The health visitor echoed this view and said she had tried to encourage Melissa to join a young mother's club that she ran but Melissa had said she did not see the point. The health visitor was, in general, fairly positive about Melissa's care of Rebecca but was concerned that she needed extra support, especially in keeping Rebecca's bottles clean. She thought it might be this that was leading to a number of stomach upsets. She was not unduly concerned, however.

Mandy agreed that it was sometimes difficult to look after Rebecca but said the best thing would be for her to have some rest by Rebecca being looked after two or three times a week.

It was agreed that Melissa harboured very negative views about her own upbringing, stating that her mother was never there for her and was too interested in her own life. She complained that Irene was now trying to meddle in her life and in her care of Rebecca.

At this point in the process, Mandy discussed with Melissa the possibility of some work with her and her mother, if Irene would agree, to re-establish the relationship and for Irene to take Melissa twice a week to give her a break. At first Melissa was dubious, thinking that this might allow Irene to become more of an influence, but she agreed to consider this as a possibility.

CASE STUDY *continued*

Part of the plan for the initial assessment had been to speak with Melissa's boyfriend but he had not been present at any of the sessions. Mandy was concerned to get an all-round view and to ensure that Irene's concerns in respect of Rebecca were considered. When Mandy finally met him she found him to be a charming and personable young man. He told her that he had been 'in care' himself as a child and he gave her permission to consult with his previous social worker. Mandy did so and was assured that he presented no cause for concern.

The initial assessment recommended family work to re-establish the relationship between Melissa and Irene, for Irene to take Rebecca twice each week – either a morning, afternoon or evening – to give Melissa a break, and for Melissa to join the health visitor's group for young mothers to gain support and advice with childcare.

Care management and assessment

We turn now to a second key area of practice, that of social work with older people, in order to help you broaden your understanding of the assessment process. Focusing on older people is an important dimension of this and the case study will be developed in subsequent chapters in the book. In order for you to develop your knowledge of assessment in this area, we have drawn on some background history and social policy context that helps to explain how the process has evolved and why particular forms of assessment have developed. We also draw your attention to the fact that the process of care management for older people is currently merging with that of the single assessment process (SAP) (Department of Health, 2002b): a multidisciplinary approach to working that is designed to prevent unnecessary delays and duplication. A key aim of SAP is to standardise the assessment processes for older people between professionals working in health and social care. An underlying principle of the 'joined up' agenda was also to promote independence for older people – a principle that has been pronounced in key policy documents such as the National Service Framework for Older People (Department of Health 2001a). Other principles which underpin the SAP are also similar to those of care management and later in this section we shall draw attention to the similarities and differences. It was the, governments intention that the single assessment process would be fully integrated on a national basis within health and social care agencies by April 2004. There have been delays and at the time of writing the SAP has not been fully integrated on a national basis. More about the slow start later.

Assessment within Adult Social Services (the statutory service for adults within local authority governance, following the structural changes resulting from the 2004 Children Act) has been evolving over the past 15 years. It is an integral part of a system known as care management which was implemented in April 1993, following the 1990 NHS and Community Care Act and linked guidance which followed. Care management is both a process and a role for practitioners and the changes brought about by the SAP build onto this process. Indeed, most social workers carrying out the revised assessments continue to be referred to as care managers. The basic principles and processes of care management that underpin current assessments have remained relatively constant. Hence they are described here in some detail.

The process includes the referral of cases and case finding, assessment, care planning, monitoring and review. These processes are important to our understanding of assessments within adult services. Underlying principles and imperatives such as resource constraints and targeting services on those with greatest need, help to explain why community care assessments (as they are officially known, but for the purposes of this text and in line with more common usage, we abbreviate to 'assessment') took a particular form and why there can be conflicting interests within the assessment frameworks. Hence at this point we give you some background information on care management. We also put down markers which point to underlying tensions that are taken up in later chapters.

Background to care management

Care management was introduced by the former Conservative government following the 1990 NHS and Community Care Act. Prior to the Act there had been criticism of the way in which community care services, particularly for older people, were organised and there was general concern that the cost of welfare provision was too high (Lewis and Glennerster, 1996). At governmental level, questions had been raised concerning the perverse incentive within community care (Audit Commission, 1986) which encouraged vulnerable older people to claim state benefits and move into private residential and nursing home accommodation. The Audit Commission held that it was cheaper to provide home based care to enable vulnerable people to remain at home where they preferred to be. However, the real price of care at home had not been fully costed since account had not been taken of the contribution made by informal carers (that is family and friends who provide the bulk of the hands-on personal care on an informal basis). In spite of this anomaly, the message from the Audit Commission that services for adults needed to be changed within the context of a commitment to community care, was well received. A key report by Sir Roy Griffiths, Community Care Agenda for Action (1988) informed and helped shape the debate. At organisational level and individual practitioner level, no one person or body seemed to be taking responsibility for community care, Griffiths described this as everybody's distant cousin but nobody's baby (page iv). The Griffiths Report, as it became known, recommended that the government should adopt a system of care management and that local authority Social Services Departments (SSD's, now Adult Social Services) should be given the responsibility for implementing what was perceived as a radical approach to delivering community care in the UK. The then Conservative government was reluctant to give additional powers to the local authorities. Nonetheless, agreement was reached and on the back of little research, and following the 1990 Act, a system of care management was adopted in local authorities with social services responsibility.

The blueprint for care management (or case management as it was then known) was spelt out in the 1989 White Paper Caring for People (Department of Health, 1989). The main aims concerned helping people to live as normal a life as possible; providing them with the right amount of care in order to promote independence; and giving them a greater say in how the services should be run in order to help them (s.1.8). The principles which underpin these aims draw on theories of normalisation, targeting and efficiency measures, and user empowerment They do not always sit comfortably together and can lead to 'tensions and ambiguities' (Postle, 2002) in the practice of care management. Nonetheless, the government was confident in its White Paper that by drawing on the skills of competent care managers the objective of making proper assessment of need ...the cornerstone of high quality care (Department of Health 1989, s.1.11.) would go some way to improving care services for adults. The optimism about this new role was apparent when, in April 1993, the 1990 Act was implemented and predominantly qualified social workers were appointed as care managers, with many moving for the first time into local authority adult services (Bradley, Manthorpe, Stanley and Alaszewski, 1996). For a fuller description of the challenges of care management see Lymbery (2005) chapter 8 'Care Management and Social Work: A Marriage Made in Heaven?'

A 'needs led' assessment in adult services

A key aspect of care management was that the process of assessment should be based on the expressed needs and preferences of the service user. Services were to be 'needs led' as opposed to being driven by services that were available to the local authority (Department of Health, 1989). Needs should be separate from and should determine the level of care and service to be provided. In order to reinforce these demarcation lines between needs led assessment and service provision, most local authorities with social services responsibility split their business. On the one hand there is the assessment and purchase of service, on the other, the provision of service. Government guidance and financial incentives have encouraged local authorities to work closely with the private, voluntary and the independent sectors in order to provide services within a mixed economy of care and move away from a market in which the former SSDs had monopolised provision. Assessment was to be based on principles of user empowerment and choice (Social Services Inspectorate (SSI) and Department of Health, 1991a). Similarly some ten years later, the 'person-centred' approach of the SAP required that 'the older person's views and wishes are central to the assessment process' (Department of Health, 2002b, annex A). However, and this is where assessment may start to become complicated, need is hard to define and it has not been defined by legislation. The guidance to managers (SSI and Department of Health, 1991b) suggested that need would vary over time as a consequence of changes in local policy and national legislation, demand at local level and the resources available. In principle therefore councils with social services responsibility can place limits on assessment by limiting the assessment of need.

Let us reflect a little on the concept of need. For a start, need is not a constant concept; it is dynamic and likely to change over time and its interpretation can be a very personal matter, dependent on personal and social expectations and influenced by the current national and local culture. For example, in the 1930s most people did not have an indoor lavatory. In some communities it was not seen as an essential need. Today attitudes have changed. The absence of an indoor loo would be viewed as an indicator of social deprivation and a public health concern. The consensus would be that the absence of such a facility would be a need that should be met within our society. Other needs may be less obvious, more open to debate and personal interpretation. For example, some older people without personal means other than the state pension may argue that society should enable them to have a hot bath or shower every day and be provided with assistance to accomplish this activity if this was required. These same people may argue that this is a personal need which they feel strongly about and which would benefit their health and quality of life. Other older people, irrespective of their financial circumstances, may view this as a luxury, not a necessity or a need that should be met by anyone other than the individual. Do you view a daily bath or shower as a necessity or luxury? If the former who should pay and/or provide the service that may be required to assist this activity? You will probably agree that perceptions of need can differ markedly between individuals. Let us look at the case of Gladys Beaumont and consider the extent to which you think (and feel) that her needs and preferences are reasonable and/or should be met by Adult Social Services.

CASE STUDY

Gladys Beaumont at home

Gladys Beaumont, is a 75-year-old widow who lives alone in a bungalow. Recently she contacted Age Concern and asked for a volunteer to visit because she said she was lonely. You, the volunteer, discover that Gladys does not go out much, apart from to the corner shop. She tells you that she 'doesn't feel steady on her legs' and that she has had diabetes for the past 20 years. Although she knows she should watch her diet, she has 'a sweet tooth and also enjoys the odd glass of sherry'. She admits that she has 'put on so much weight' and adds, defiantly 'but why not – I have so few pleasures?'

You're not an expert but you think that Gladys' diet and size are probably making her condition worse. You start to visit on a weekly basis. Most of the visits conclude with Gladys telling you that her 'heart's desire' is to be looked after, since she is weary of living alone. She asks you to contact 'the welfare' so that a place could be found for her in 'a home'. However, she does not want to continue to live in Northham where she was born, an industrial town that is miles from the coast. Rather, she wants to move to a residential home on the Isle of Wight and have a room with a sea view. Her one contact there is an old school friend with whom she exchanges Christmas cards. When asked how she would fund this, Gladys says she has no savings, but then adds feistily 'the welfare should pay – I've paid my dues'.

ACTIVITY 1.3

1. *Do you think Gladys' 'needs' are reasonable? List some of the reasons for and against.*

2. *Write down the reasons why you think Gladys should be helped by her local Adult Social Services to fulfil her 'heart felt' needs.*

3. *Write down the reasons why you think this may not be the role for Adult Social Services.*

There are no absolute answers to the activity above. Some, but probably not many people may consider Gladys as eligible for residential care (more about eligibility later). However, if she were eligible for nursing or residential care she could choose the location of the home and her funding authority would pay subject to means testing, the normal costs.

The learning point here is that your personal and political values and preferences are likely to determine how you think and feel about Gladys Beaumont's needs. Perhaps you could spend some time reflecting on the type of values which you drew on to form your opinion of Gladys' needs. Being clear about your own values, and recognising the extent to which personal values may affect professional judgement and practice, is an important part of developing your assessment skills (Bradley and Manthorpe, 1997 Banks 2004).

Care management and the process of assessment

Local authorities, under section 47 of the NHS and Community Care Act 1990, have a legal duty to assess needs for community care services:

> *s.47...where it appears to a local authority that any person for whom they may provide or arrange for the provision of community care services may be in need of any such services, the authority –*
>
> *(a) shall carry out an assessment of his needs for those services; and*
>
> *(b) having regard to the results of the assessment, shall decide whether his needs call for the provision by them of any such services.*

It is important to underline the point that in terms of the community care legislation, the legal duty is primarily to assess where there is an appearance of need. This is not the same as assessment on request. Further, other requirements of Adult Social Services are not laid down by legal statute, and are conveyed to local authorities through government guidance and circulars. As such, these documents are not as powerful and are more open to interpretation and local discretion. For further details of the legal position of the community care legislation and its impact on care management we suggest you read Johns (2007), and Brayne and Carr (2005) Chapter 16, Community and residential care (see *References* section for full details).

Initial assessments within care management start at the level of enquiry or referral to the agency, since the basic information taken by reception staff significantly determines the type of assessment that is triggered. It may be the case that an assessment is not triggered at this point following initial screening. If the level of need is thought to be high then a care manager is allocated to undertake an assessment. Guidance put forward by the government for practitioners (SSI and Department of Health, 1991, pages 47–56) suggested that care managers should approach their work in a sequence similar to the following ten steps:

1. Negotiate the scope of the assessment – based on the 'least that is necessary to know' principle; practitioners are advised to proceed in ways that are simple, speedy and as informal as possible (page 47).

2. Find the appropriate setting – ideally one which is most relaxing for service user – likely to be own home.

3. Clarify expectation – ensuring that users understand what is involved; likely timescale; authority vested in care manager; possible outcomes; and users' entitlement to information, participation and representation (page 49).

4. Promote participation – users and carers to be encouraged to participate to the limit of their capacity (page 51).

5. Establish a relationship of trust – by drawing on helping skills of listening, observing and understanding (page 52).

6. Assess need – guided by the user's view of the problem, the care manager needs to: clarify the cause of the problem(s); avoid wide ranging assessments; strive to reach a consensus; record and acknowledge different views of the problem, whilst noting that *the assessing practitioner is responsible for defining user's needs* and for *distinguishing facts from interpretation* (page 53).

7. Determine eligibility – linked to policy statements that trigger intervention and resources, for example the user's level of risk, ability to self-care and type of social context. (see eligibility criteria and fair access to care on page 34).

8. Set priorities – and rank in terms of practitioner/agency priority and those deemed important by the service user.

9. Agree objectives – and how these can be achieved.

10. Record the assessment of need and share with the service user.

The single assessment process (SAP)

In the NHS Plan (Department of Health, 2000a) and in the National Service Framework (NSF) for Older People (Department of Health, 2001a), the government proposed the introduction of the SAP. As mentioned earlier, this process helps standardise the assessment of older people, between professionals working in similar and complementary fields. By introducing the SAP, the government is responding to many of the criticisms aimed at multidisciplinary working within the context of care management (Manthorpe, Stanley, Bradley and Alaszewski, 1996; Quinney, 2006). The aim of the SAP is *to promote better care services and better outcomes for older people, and more effective use of professional resources*. Particularly the SAP *should ensure that the scale and depth of assessment is kept in proportion to older people's needs, agencies do not duplicate each other's assessments, and professionals contribute to assessments in the most effective way* (Department of Health 2002b section on *Guidance for Local Implementation*, page 1).

Local stakeholders, including older people, service users, carers, providers, other local statutory agencies such as housing, and local voluntary organisations should be involved in drawing up plans for the local implementation of the SAP, based on the 12 steps which will build onto and expand the assessment process in care management as described above. We include a brief description of these steps in order to give you an overview of the assessment culture for older people in health and social care as follows. (For a fuller appraisal of the steps see Department of Health, 2002b, annex A–J, pages 1–42.)

1. Local agencies to agree purpose and outcome of SAP – by consulting widely and focusing on potential benefits such as minimising duplication of effort amongst a range of professionals and reducing paperwork by providing a single assessment summary – the collecting and sharing of information to be based on the informed consent of the older person.

2. Agree shared values between agencies – see Department of Health, 2002b, annex D.

3. Agencies to agree terminology and reach a common language – by referring to e.g. definitions in the NSF for Older People.

4. Map care processes – agencies to map how older people currently move through the system from point of entry, to delivery of service and note how assessment processes link to the single assessment.

5. Agencies to estimate the types and numbers of older people needing assessment.

6. Agencies agree the stages of assessment and care management to cover: publishing information about services; completing four types of assessment: i contact assessment – this refers to the first contact between the older person and agency and the point

where basic personal information is recorded; ii <u>overview assessment</u> – is carried out by health and social care professionals when a 'more rounded' assessment is needed to explore aspects such as personal care, physical well-being, mental health. Professional judgement and the wishes of the service user will dictate the scope and scale of this assessment. iii An overview assessment may trigger a <u>specialist assessment</u> – used to explore specific needs, drawing on the expertise and judgement of a range of qualified health and social care staff such as social workers, old age psychiatrists. iv A <u>comprehensive assessment</u> – offered to service users where level of treatment and support is intensive and prolonged, e.g. complex and extensive home based care packages; evaluate assessment information; decide on the help to be offered, drawing on eligibility criteria; care planning; monitoring; and review. Annex E provides detailed guidance on each stage of assessment.

7. Agree the link between medical diagnosis and assessment.

8. Agree the domains and sub-domains of assessment e.g. within the domain of *personal care and physical well-being* the sub-domains are likely to include personal hygiene, ability to dress, mobility and sleep patterns (see Annex F).

9. Agree common assessment approaches, tools and scales (see Annex C, for criteria for evaluating local approaches to assessment and implementation milestones).

10. Agree joint working arrangements for assessment and care planning – being clear about practitioner and agency responsibility and statutory duties (statutory duties are summarised in Annex E under 'legal matters').

11. Agree a single assessment summary; how it should be collected, stored and shared taking into consideration for example the Data Protection Act and informed consent.

12. Implement a joint staff development strategy (see Annex J.)

When producing guidance on the SAP the Department of Health were not envisaging radical change, since they were aware that many of the structures were already in place within care management. In preparation for the implementation of the SAP in April 2004 nominal guidance was issued (Department of Health, 2004) that principally reinforced and upheld the 2002 guidance. The 12 step guidance as described provides the framework for a successful implementation. It was also emphasised that a key to a consistent approach was the way in which assessment information, subject to consent of the service user, was stored and shared, using the Single Assessment Summary or local equivalent as described in Annex I (Department of Health, 2002b). This Annex was modified in November 2003. The need for appropriate training of professionals to enable them to carry out person-centred assessments and care planning (see Annex J. Department of Health, 2002b) was reinforned and examples of good practice in the early implementation of the SAP were cited in a range of local authorities (Department of Health, 2004).

The government appeared confident in the White Paper 'Our health, our care our say' (Department of Health, 2006) that work on the SAP had been well developed and that initiatives were underway to build on this and develop a Common Assessment Framework 'to ensure less duplication across different agencies and allow people to self assess where possible' (page 115).

Slow start to SAP

In practice the SAP is still 'bedding in' and there has been a level of drift in its implementation, that may be a reflection on the priority given to this process at national and local level. Indeed, it was the government's intention that the implementation of SAP would be cost neutral and this has been met with a healthy scepticism (McNally et al., 2003). Anecdotal information indicates that practitioners are finding that the contact and overview assessments have a tendency to promote 'social work by numbers'. The forms are seen as extensive, health dominated and focus on a 'need to know' basis rather than a holisitic assessment. The first professional person who visits the service user in his/her home is normally required to fill in the appropriate sections, but this does not always happen. Some are wary of disclosing sensitive information on the service user (for example financial information) that is usually left in a brightly coloured folder in a conspicuous place in the home. There is also the challenge created by professional differences and the meanings given to different terminology, for example that of care planning (Griffiths, 2006). Progress has also been hampered by the fact that not all authorities have a shared data base and/or compatible electronic systems. On the other hand, local authority care managers can see the benefits of sharing assessments with allied professionals: in the old system the task normally fell to them and they were not always the best person to do this work.

We turn once more to the case of Gladys Beaumont to give you an opportunity to test out your learning of some of the assessment skills which you have absorbed so far. Read the following case details and answer the questions at the end.

CASE STUDY

Gladys Beaumont in hospital

Eighteen months later, Gladys' situation has changed. She is currently on a surgical ward in the local hospital recovering from a below the knee amputation. She had known that her difficulty in walking was due, in part, to poor blood circulation, which was somehow linked to her diabetes, but she had put the acute pains in her toes down to chilblains. She was shocked therefore to discover that it was gangrene and not chilblains. The district nurse, Samantha Smith, has been visiting regularly for several months and providing treatment, but the disease has spread. Gladys had been dismissive of the care manager who visited a year ago from the local Adult Social Services, when she was told she was 'not eligible for care' and thus it was unlikely that a move to a residential home on the Isle of Wight would be funded by her local Adult Social Services. She had also been outraged when she was given a list of agencies who provide cleaning at £10 per hour. She was also dismissive of weekly daycare 'to reduce her social isolation' as the care manager put it – and particularly since she would have to pay for it. That same day she had asked her neighbour Janice Brown to help and she seemed more than willing.

Following her operation, her general level of fitness and weight has not helped Gladys to mobilise well. The physiotherapist, Andrea Monroe, is not confident that she will learn to walk with a prosthesis (a false leg). Even if she had a wheelchair she argues that she would not at this point be independent since she is not 'weight bearing' on her good limb and thus not able to 'transfer her weight' and move herself, for example, from bed to wheelchair. Similarly the occupational therapist, Judith Ward, is doubtful whether she *could cope alone at home. She has had some visitors but appears to have few close family or friends. Gladys is very upset about the loss of her limb. Propped up in bed Gladys is waiting to see, with some apprehension, the hospital based care manager, Sarah Jacobs.*

ACTIVITY **1.4**

Put yourself in the role of the care manager based on the ward.

Drawing on what you have learned about good practice in both care management and the single assessment process, together with what you have learned so far about assessment in this chapter, how would you go about enabling Gladys to share her story with you and constructing an assessment of her needs?

Where should the assessment take place and why?

Who do you think should be involved?

Again, there are no absolute answers to these questions. You may wish to take the guidance set out for care management as your starting point or you may wish to consider ways in which a 'joint narrative' or story can be developed. The process will help you to identify some of the values you bring to the task of assessment. Look at the sequel which we describe later in the chapter to see how we might approach the case.

Eligibility criteria and fair access to care services

An important element of the assessment, and one which many would argue captured the spirit of the care management culture, is that of targeting assessment and resources on those people with the greatest needs. In order to fulfil the targeting imperative, local authorities with responsibilities for adult services have been steered by government to implement assessment criteria, known as 'eligibility criteria'. These are scales in which levels of dependency are described in order of need and risk. The categories are then matched with a service users's profile of need as determined in the assessment. As indicated, eligibility criteria remains under the SAP.

The early recommendation was that the full eligibility scale should be used, and thus, for example, service users located in bands that indicated lower risk would receive 'simple' or 'standard' services. Many authorities focused their attention, however, on service users in the high risk eligibility band where stricter eligibility criteria have been used for certain adult service users. Ten years on, the government was concerned that different local authorities were using different eligibility criteria (Local Authority Circular (LAC) 2002, 13, Department of Health, 2002c) which resulted in inconsistency in terms of access to social care for adults and pointed to a national system which was unfair. Lack of parity in the system had been compounded by practices in some local authorities where eligibility criteria were used for both assessment and for a particular service and where stricter eligibility criteria had been used for certain adult service users. As a consequence the government has set a national eligibility framework based on risks that are linked with various forms of disability, impairment and difficulty. The guidance on eligibility prioritises the risks faced by individuals into four bands that describe the seriousness of the risk which if not addressed will affect, for example, independence. The bands are – critical, substantial, moderate and low, as detailed below (details of the bands have been taken directly from the Department of Health website 2003a).

Critical – when

- Life is, or will be, threatened.

- And/or significant health problems have developed or will develop.

- And/or there is, or will be, little or no choice and control over vital aspects of the immediate environment.

- And/or serious abuse or neglect has occurred or will occur.

- And/or there is, or will be, an inability to carry out vital personal care or domestic routines.

- And/or vital involvement in work, education or learning cannot or will not be sustained.

- And/or vital social support systems and relationships cannot or will not be sustained.

- And/or vital family and other social roles and responsibilities cannot or will not be undertaken.

Substantial – when

- There is, or will be, only partial choice and control over the immediate environment.

- And/or abuse or neglect has occurred or will occur.

- And/or there is, or will be, an inability to carry out the majority of personal care or domestic routines.

- And/or involvement in many aspects of work, education or learning cannot or will not be sustained.

- And/or the majority of social support systems and relationships cannot or will not be sustained.

- And/or the majority of family and other social roles and responsibilities cannot or will not be undertaken.

Moderate – when

- There is, or will be, an inability to carry out several personal care or domestic routines.

- And/or involvement in several aspects of work, education or learning cannot or will not be sustained.

- And/or several social support systems and relationships cannot or will not be sustained.

- And/or several family and other social roles and responsibilities cannot or will not be undertaken.

Low – when

- There is, or will be, an inability to carry out one or two personal care or domestic routines.

- And/or involvement in one or two aspects of work, education or learning cannot or will not be sustained.

- And/or one or two social support systems and relationships cannot or will not be sustained.

- And/or one or two family and other social roles and responsibilities cannot or will not be undertaken.

As part of the *Fair Access to Care Services* (Department of Health, 2002b), local authorities were charged to review their eligibility criteria by April 2003 in consultation with *local stakeholders including current service users, NHS bodies and other appropriate local organisations* (page 2). In implementing the new guidance, local authorities are allowed to take into consideration their resources available for adult services. This point has been reinforced in the SAP guidance (Department of Health, 2002b, annex E). The government recognises that, as a consequence, services may differ between localities, but the aspiration is that *people with similar needs (are) to be assured of similar care outcomes.* Resource issues within care management are a significant aspect (see section on financing care plans for adults in Chapter 3).

We return once more to Gladys Beaumont and describe the sequel to the case which includes a multidisciplinary home visit in order to help you to build up a profile and understanding of her assessment and her likely eligibility banding.

CASE STUDY

Gladys Beaumont – assessment – the multidisciplinary home visit

Gladys had been pleasantly surprised by the warmth and sensitivity of Sarah Jacobs, the care manager on the ward, and has felt comfortable discussing practical as well as personal details and aspects of her life which she has rarely discussed before. Until the hospital admission Gladys had not seen her neighbour, Janice Brown, in her true light. Janice has been her most regular visitor and not just brief 'courtesy calls' such as that of her niece Anthea Jones.

Gladys has been profoundly shocked by the amputation of her limb. In this heightened state of awareness she has seen things differently. Discussions with Sarah have led her to recognise several 'home truths'. She is now resolved to take more care of her health and diet. Having had time to reflect she no longer thinks that the 'grass is greener' somewhere else. Northham and her bungalow are home and Gladys positively wants to return home and do things that she has not done for a long time, such as attend the church and visit the local park. It seems that now that an independent and active life is more difficult, she values it more highly (for a fuller description of Gladys's response to social work intervention see the section on crisis management in Chapter 4).

Sarah has described the care management process to Gladys and shown her the assessment forms which she has been gradually completing in Gladys' presence and in her full knowledge. Although Sarah is pleased with Gladys' attitude to her rehabilitation, and recognises that her living accommodation in a bungalow is a definite plus, she remains concerned about Gladys' ability to live alone once more. Her concern has been triggered by the assessments of the occupational therapist and physiotherapist. They have outlined substantial concerns about her current mobility and ability to lead an independent life alone at home. Gladys is still not fully 'weight bearing' and cannot transfer herself for example from bed to wheelchair and continues to need extensive physiotherapy. Her disability affects her level of self-care and competence in daily living skills and she is having to relearn how to do basic tasks, such as boil a kettle from a wheelchair position. Given her general health, Gladys will also require regular care and support if she is to make progress.

The home visit

Gladys had agreed to a home visit with key staff from the ward, people involved in her care, Janice her neighbour, Samantha Smith the district nurse and Matthew Priest from the local Adult Social Services, who will be responsible for constructing and implementing the care plan when she leaves hospital. Gladys knows that on the home visit she will try to put into practice what she has learned whilst in hospital, so that the professionals and friend involved in her care can help her to make decisions, the detail of which will form the care plan.

On the visit Gladys is the focus of attention and the multidisciplinary team assess the extent to which she will be independent at home and the risks that may be involved. Whilst she can get about the kitchen in her wheelchair and prepare hot drinks and light snacks for herself, she is still not secure moving from bed to wheelchair or managing personal care tasks, such as dressing, bathing and toileting. Matthew is wary of committing his team's stretched resources when Gladys is not able, for example, to go to the bathroom independently, but is aware that she meets his local authority's eligibility criteria and that he therefore has a duty to provide a service. Gladys is also adamant that she will not go to bed before 10 p.m., even though the 'putting to bed service' does not operate due to staff shortages after 9 p.m. Matthew suggests that she should be kept in hospital longer for more intensive rehabilitation. Gladys steadfastly refuses saying that she will make a quicker recovery at home. Samantha, the district nurse, suggests that she has a catheter (a tubular instrument passed into the bladder to draw urine, which is collected into a bag that needs emptying regularly) fitted in order to address one of the key problems. Gladys refused since there are no medical reasons to have a catheter and she knows (from a friend who has one) that it can cause infections. Janice offers to put her to bed, but there are doubts expressed by several present that this may be exploitative of the neighbour's good will and may not be sustainable. Nonetheless in his assessment of the banding Matthew takes the informal care on offer into account.

Gladys cannot see that she may be at a high level of risk living alone at home and that she will require significant assistance in order to continue to live by herself. She thinks Matthew is being overly cautious in his assessment of the banding which is as follows:

(a) level of self-care: substantial;

(b) daily living skills: substantial;

(c) mobility: critical;

(d) general health and disabling conditions: substantial.

ACTIVITY **1.5**

From the information disclosed so far, give your reasons why you think Matthew has 'banded' Gladys as indicated (see details of the four bands provided above). Conversely, if you disagree with Matthew's assessment explain your reasoning.

If you are able to share this activity with a colleague it will help you to identify some of the complex issues involved in determining eligibility and a person's needs. It is clear that the criteria and guidance set by the Department of Health need to be applied with skill and artistry to be effective. Undertaking this activity will also help you to recognise the centrality of values and ethics for good social work practice.

ACTIVITY **1.6**

How hospital and area based care managers co-ordinate their work is often a consequence of local arrangements. In this concluding activity in the first chapter we ask you to find out how similar care managers in your own locality work together. We also ask you to reflect on whether you think the reasons they give for co-ordinating/transferring work in a particular way is in the best interest of the service user.

C H A P T E R   S U M M A R Y

In this chapter, you have been introduced to some of the complexities involved in social work assessments. Different understandings and approaches have been introduced and the importance of working together with service users and carers has been promoted. By way of helping you to meet relevant aspects of the National Occupational Standards case studies have been developed. You have been able to consider how to assess needs and options and recommend a course of action, the importance of written assessments, assessing risk and using your knowledge to assess as part of a wider social work process that involves planning, intervention and review. In the next chapter we will explore a range of helpful techniques to assist you in developing the skills to make effective assessment. Whenever you are involved in assessment work, ask yourself the following questions.

- What information do you think you need?

- Why do you think this is important?

- How will you collect it?

- How will you make sure that service users are involved at all stages?

- How will you construct an assessment report from this information?

- What skills are involved in undertaking an assessment?

- Write a plan describing what you intend to do on an assessment visit.

- What ethical considerations do you need to take into account when conducting a social work assessment?

It is also important to bear in mind the following:

- know why you are making an assessment;

- know the reasons why your agency makes assessments and to what purpose an assessment will or might be put;

- plan carefully for all assessments;

- be aware of the power you have as a social worker;

- check your assessments carefully with service users and others contributing to the process;

- treat the information gained with care and sensitivity – know the bounds and limits of confidentiality.

FURTHER READING

Department of Health, Department for Education and Employment, Home Office (2000) Framework for the assessment of children in need and their families. London: The Stationery Office.

The Framework provides a comprehensive introduction to assessment in childcare social work, paying attention to theory, practice and the interprofessional context in which social workers practise.

Lymbery, M (2005) Social Work with Older People Context Policy and Practice. London, Sage Publications.

Drawing on current policy and practice this book provides informal and realistic options for working with older people.

Middleton, L (1997) The art of assessment. Birmingham: Venture Press.

This accessible book provides a helpful overview of models of assessment. It is practical and focuses on social work as practised in the UK.

Milner, J and O'Byrne, P (2002) Assessment in social work. 2nd edition. Basingstoke: Palgrave.

This book provides an in-depth and critical treatment of assessment, highlighting the central importance of anti-discriminatory practice and values for social workers undertaking assessment.

Social Services Inspectorate and Department of Health (1991) Care management and assessment: practitioners' guide. London: HMSO.

This work gives detailed guidance for the practitioner on the process of care management, particularly that of assessment, care planning, monitoring and reviewing.

Chapter 2

Tools and diagrammatic aids to assessment

Introduction

There are a number of aids, activities and tools that can be employed to gather and represent the data social workers may collect in order to complete initial and ongoing assessments. In this chapter, we shall consider five particular tools that can help in making assessments and beginning to analyse information collected from service users and carers. These are:

- genograms;
- ecomaps;
- culturagrams;
- flow charts;
- life road maps (the latter two will be considered together).

Making an assessment is not a value-neutral activity and your prior experiences, thoughts and beliefs will influence the process and your understanding of the information gathered. Therefore, it is helpful to ask yourself the following questions throughout this chapter:

- Why am I collecting this information?
- To what purposes will this information be put?
- How would I react if asked to undertake these activities?

It is also important to keep the person using social work services at the heart of the assessment as we have seen in chapter one. It will help, therefore, to ask yourself '*how can I best include the person requesting or receiving a service?*' At times throughout the section you will be asked to complete activities about your own family, lifestyle and networks. Undertaking this work may raise issues that you have not thought about before or trigger quite deep-seated feelings. Be prepared for this and, if you are affected, seek some support from colleagues, friends or other trusted people. Remember, assessment is not an emotionally neutral area and professionals are human beings too. If you are challenged in some ways by information about your family and life, consider how much greater these feelings might be for someone who is volunteering this information in a social work relationship. We are not using our developing case studies relating to Rebecca and her family or Gladys Beaumont to illustrate these models in this chapter but another case study. This is to demonstrate the versatility of the tools. At the end of this chapter you will be asked to review what you have learned by applying your knowledge to what you know about either Rebecca and her family or Gladys.

Genograms

The uses of genograms

A genogram is a type of family tree. It provides an immediate visual representation of the individual or family being assessed. It is a 'snapshot' of how that person or family is structured and viewed at a particular moment in time. As such, it can be useful in highlighting to social workers those areas that may cause concern, and information that is lacking and needs to be sought. It may also identify areas or themes for further exploration with the service user. Furthermore, as it is a family tree, it presents an historical picture or document from which the social worker can gain insight into a variety of patterns regularly occurring within that family unit and that may still influence the way in which that family operates. Thus, as Hartman (1995) states, the genogram can be useful in portraying the family unit across time.

Genograms are not undertaken solely for the benefit of social workers, however. Using genograms is a participative activity that can help you to form a working relationship with service users. This is, of course, beneficial in forming constructive working alliances, and encouraging the development of service users' motivations to work with you. Involvement in an interactive and practical activity, which compiling a genogram can be, may help to reduce nervousness and anxiety by placing something between the service user and yourself as a social work practitioner. This can act as a focus of attention rather than the people compiling the genogram. Being actively involved in the genogram's construction may enable service users to feel better as a result of 'doing something'. This active approach can help to restore confidence in one's ability to take a degree of control in one's life. It has the additional benefit of helping the service user to recognise patterns, to face difficult areas and to consider their family history as a process in which they are intimately involved. Hodge (2005) adds an important perspective to the use of genograms, and other tools, to assess spiritual needs. Unfortunately, his paper does associate spirituality rather too easily with religious belief but genograms can be used to identify these belief systems and patterns important to those families and individuals completing them.

The construction of a genogram is a fairly simple task. However, it can be a very powerful process and may raise a number of varying emotions within those completing the task. The social worker needs to be mindful of this and to be sensitive to the emotions of the subject. This, of course, can add to the assessment process. An additional benefit of the genogram can be its capacity to engender discussion and to raise important issues that social workers need to deal with and which may not have been recognised or the opportunity to explore would not have arisen if the activity had not been undertaken. However, this cannot be done at the expense of the service user's level of comfort with the process. The pace of the work must take its lead from the service user, and, especially in the case of children and young people, it must take into account the age and development of the service user. People will need time to assimilate information about themselves, their lives and families. The social worker who allows this time is likely to be appreciated by service users for respecting their feelings and situations. This can add to the development of a positive working relationship.

Symbols used in developing genograms

There are a number of almost universally accepted symbols used in the compilation of genograms. These can be found in most books concerning systemic family therapy, but an especially good point of reference is McGoldrick, Gerson and Shellenberger (1999), which details the many different symbols and indicators to be used. The most common symbols are shown below.

◯ female

☐ male

△ unknown gender (pregnancy)

✝ death

◯—☐ enduring relationship (marriage/cohabitation)

◯----☐ transitory relationship

◯—/—☐ separation

◯—//—☐ divorce

Genogram symbols

The relationship between generations is shown by lines connecting parents to children. This is shown in the following diagram that includes further common symbols used in genograms.

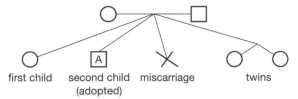

first child second child miscarriage twins
(adopted)

Developing connections and relationships using genograms

When collecting the information and compiling the genogram with the service user, it is important that you collect full names, dates of birth, and the exact dates of significant events within the family life history. Asking service users for the dates when their parents married, divorced, or when grandparents died, the dates of separations and divorces, dates of marriages, or having children helps to map out significant historical events and contextualises them. This is important for the social worker and equally important for the subjects of the genogram. However, it is not always easy to ask questions about the intimate details of a person's life or family. Sometimes using a genogram can help the social worker overcome these difficulties and ensure that a comprehensive assessment has been undertaken.

Assume, for instance, that you are working with the Pritchard family and their concerns about Tom their second child who is adopted. Eleanor and James Pritchard are worried that Tom is not settling in with the family. You have been asked to make an assessment of their current situation and have begun to compile a genogram. You have explained to the family that in order to help with their situation in the best possible way you will need to look widely at the family, its history, composition and present situation. Eleanor and James agreed, being aware of assessments from their adoption of Tom. Constructing a genogram can be an interactive activity that helps families and social workers engage with one another. Therefore, you might ask James and Eleanor to draw their family situation. Let us consider that the following information is provided.

Married 1990

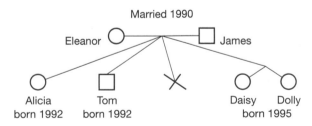

Eleanor James

Alicia Tom Daisy Dolly
born 1992 born 1992 born 1995

James and Eleanor

You note that the date of Tom's adoption is not mentioned nor is the date of the miscarriage. Also, there is no information about James' or Eleanor's parents or siblings or, indeed, dates of birth. In identifying this missing information you are formulating possible further questions to ask or avenues to explore. In this case it would be helpful to point to some of the missing information. Perhaps you might say 'I see you have put down Tom's year of birth, and it is the same as Alicia's. However, I wonder if you could tell me when he was adopted?' You may also wish to ask directly if James and Eleanor have any brothers or sisters, and about their parents.

In asking for this factual information you will then be in a position to search more deeply: to look at the involvement of grandparents, uncles and aunts in the life of the family. This depends on the information being gathered and as a social worker you need to develop the skills to determine where, when and how questions should be asked. As a start, the genogram allows you to identify gaps in information and clarify your understanding.

It can be hard to ask difficult and personal questions but harder still to answer them. Remembering this when making an assessment will help. It is useful to acknowledge how difficult it might be to answer a question when asking it. If, for instance, you wanted to know a little more about Eleanor's miscarriage and how it might have impacted on the family, you might ask 'I recognise that this might be a difficult thing to talk about, but you have included having a miscarriage in your genogram. Could you tell me when that happened?' Depending on the answer, and how it was conveyed, you may wish to explore matters further.

Imagine that your questions provided the following information: Eleanor had a miscarriage in 1993; Eleanor's parents both died in a car crash in 1980 when she was 13. This was six years before she and James met in 1986 when she was 19 and he was 20 years old. Eleanor was an only child. James' parents were still alive and were involved in the family. However, since Tom's adoption in 1999 they had tended to argue more with James and Eleanor and were convinced that they were 'storing up trouble' by adopting Tom. His difficulties settling down at home and reports of unacceptable behaviour at school confirmed their view to James' parents. James' brother and partner were described as very supportive. The genogram had brought more information to light that could be used to help Tom settle into the family. The genogram itself now looked like this:

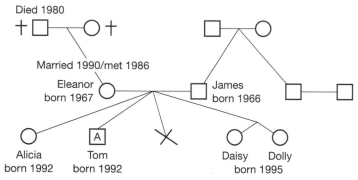

James and Eleanor across three generations

Genograms in family therapy

Burnham (1986) and Hartman (1995), working from a systemic perspective, are extremely relevant to this discussion. The use of the genogram is debated in these texts. Barker (1986) places genograms in the context of assessment prior to intervening with whole families in a therapeutic context. He places the genogram in the wider perspective of family assessment. In his work, he reviews one of the key models family workers have employed in assessing the functioning of families – the circumplex model, which examines how cohesive or adaptable family members are. Barker (1986) also considers a range of different assessment models. The genogram contributes to whichever model of assessment is employed. It is now considered central to working in child and family social work, when undertaking comprehensive assessments.

Given the range of emotions that may surface and the potential for uncovering previously unconsidered patterns in one's family history, it is important for the social worker to have some idea of how this may feel for service users. By completing the following activity, you will have a chance to explore some of these emotions.

ACTIVITY 2.1

Using the symbols outlined above, construct your own genogram. Do this for at least three generations in your family. You can place yourself at any generational level depending upon your circumstances. For instance, if you are the child in your genogram, you will need to include grandparents and parents. If you are a parent you might be 'sandwiched' between your parents and your children. However, if you place yourself at the grandparent level please include a fourth level to indicate your parents. This will give a sense of change over history.

When you have completed your genogram examine it closely for patterns or norms of behaviour or event. Some examples may help here:

- *If there are no separations or divorces in your family history does this suggest an unspoken rule about commitment to relationships?*

- *If daughters tend not to marry/cohabit until late does this explain the hostility to your sister leaving home to live with a partner at the age of 18?*

- *Might the family approach to death and bereavement be influenced by the fact that males have tended to die in their early 60s, whilst females have lived until their late 80s?*

Think about how the process of constructing the genogram made you feel. Was it sometimes an emotional and painful experience? In what ways was this painful, exciting or simply informative and interesting? Can you think of some ways in which some of the strong emotions that may be raised when constructing a genogram can be ameliorated? Did you discover things about your family and your own attitudes and values that now seem more understandable? How does this make you feel?

Common reactions and thoughts often reflect a mix of sadness when thinking of relatives who may have died or relationships that have ended as well as enjoyment and fascination when learning things about one's own family. Perhaps some of the ways in which painful memories can be ameliorated include having another person with you to share feelings with, by writing down thoughts about losses, by slowing the pace or by leaving aside aspects of one's family history until feeling more comfortable. Olsen et al. (2004) extend the use of genograms into areas of health which may be of increasing importance when undertaking multidisciplinary assessments which feature highly in contemporary practice.

By attempting this activity you may learn ways of using genograms in sensitive and empowering ways with service users, as well as for the professional purpose of collecting and analysing information. You may wish to write down your answers and add to them as you complete this chapter.

The following case study demonstrates some of the uses of a genogram in both collecting information and beginning to establish an understanding of situations in which people find themselves. This is something that needs to happen before being able to plan and intervene to bring about change.

Damien Jones was referred by his mother who was concerned that he seemed to spend long periods on his own and was not developing in the same way as her other two children. Given this scant information it was necessary to make arrangements to conduct a comprehensive assessment of the situation. At the first interview a social and personal history was taken. Part of this process was achieved by the compilation of a genogram. In the first instance this was done to help elucidate the composition of the family. It was explained to Mrs Jones that it was important to see the family as a whole and to consider how Damien fitted in.

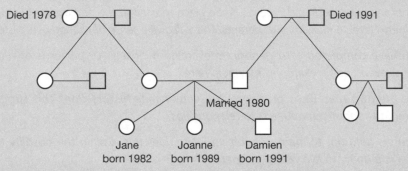

Damien Jones

During the course of the interview it transpired that Mrs Jones was, in fact, concerned that her mother-in-law appeared to favour the other two children and to ignore Damien. The genogram helped the social worker to question in a focused manner and to make a hypothesis relating to the death of Damien's grandfather in 1991 and his birth. It is not always the case that such hypotheses work. However, in this particular case it was found that Damien was born only one week after the death of his grandfather. This had led to several ramifications in an otherwise fairly well functioning family. Mrs Jones had enjoyed a good relationship with her mother-in-law who had helped with the care of Jane and Joanne over a number of years, especially during the pregnancy with Damien. During this pregnancy Mrs Jones had been quite ill and, at times was incapacitated. Mr Jones' mother helped out when it was not possible for him to take time off from work. Unfortunately, Mr Jones' father became ill and, after only a short illness, died. Mrs Jones' mother-in-law now blamed her for being ill when her husband was ill, and Damien served as a constant reminder of her bereavement. As a result Mrs Jones no longer received help from her mother-in-law, and when she did visit she ignored Damien whilst lavishing attention on Jane and Joanne. The increased demands on her time meant that Mrs Jones herself could not spend as much time with Damien as she had with her other two children, and, upon further exploration, she felt guilty about this.

The genogram taken in this case study provided useful visual information, an opportunity to form a working hypothesis, and it created an atmosphere conducive to frank and open discussion. It did not say anything directly about the networks of support available and utilised by the family, however. This information had to be sought, initially, from careful questioning. A way of gathering such information in a visual way is contained in the ecomap. It is to this particular assessment tool that we will now turn.

The genogram interview

McGoldrick, Gerson and Shellenberger (1999) provide a useful outline model for an interview in which information for a genogram is gathered or in which a genogram is compiled together with a family. The information gathered is purposive and concerns interactions as well as relationships within families. They suggest that social workers start with the presenting problem and move on to consider the current living situation of family members and family history. They suggest the following questions are helpful:

- Why are they coming for help now?
- When did the problem begin?
- Who noticed it?
- How does each person view it?
- How has each responded?
- What were relations like prior to the problem?
- Has the problem changed? How?
- What will happen if it continues?

During the interview social workers will explore rituals, beliefs and expectations within those families with whom they are working. McGoldrick et al. (1999) see the genogram as part of the process of working towards change and include service user strengths to enable an analysis of the information and potential for change. Other suggested questions include the following:

- Who lives in the household (names, ages, gender)?
- How is each related?
- Where do other members live?
- Were there any similar problems in the family before?
- What solutions were tried in the past (therapy, treatment, hospitalisation etc)?
- What has been happening recently in the family?
- Have there been any recent changes or stressors?

Ecomaps

The genogram placed the family in a temporal context demonstrating its links with history and connections across and between generations. The ecomap is another visual representation useful in assessment and analysis but locates the family and/or individual members within it in a spatial context; it looks at the networks available in the environment in which the person using social work services lives. These networks may represent individuals or organisations and agencies with whom service users interact. To reflect the focus on social networks, Coulshed and Orme (2006) refer to them explicity as 'network maps'.

Based as it is upon systems thinking, the ecomap seeks to show the various connections and interrelations between a range of systems and sub-systems involved with the family and/or individual members. This means that an ecomap seeks to show how family members act and react to each other and how the family as a whole relates to other families, groups and organisations in society. It also can be used to demonstrate interrelations between various levels within environmental living systems. A visual representation of the way systems and sub-systems interact may be helpful here.

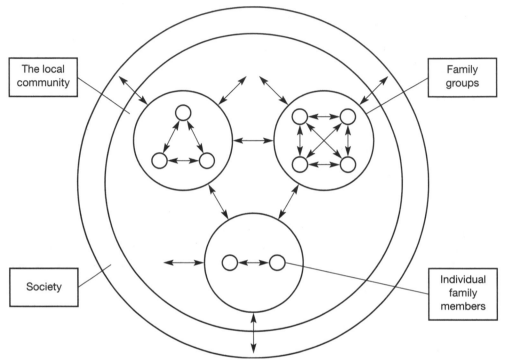

Systems and the ways they might relate

This diagram may look, at first glance, very complex. However, it shows the different levels at which individuals and families interact on an everyday basis, considering the influences that come from individuals and families and in return have an impact upon them. For instance, individual family members have a mutual or reciprocal influence on one another, but in turn each family member is influenced by and has an influence on other individuals, families and organisations with whom they have contact. They are also influenced by wider society, portrayals of issues in the media and social policy issues of the day. Part of this wider social view itself stems from the collective influence that individuals have on each other and on the development of wider 'common-sense' or shared understandings.

In the same way that genograms can help the process of engagement with families, so too can the use of ecomaps. Ecomaps provide an 'at-a-glance' perspective, showing who is involved with whom and in what ways. They are participative and can foster constructive discussion during their compilation if undertaken together. For instance, the following question may result from using ecomaps with families *Why is it that one member of the family feels that the next-door-neighbour represents their strongest support whilst other members of the family believe her support comes with a high degree of stress?* Compiling ecomaps as a family unit can also encourage debate and discussion concerning beliefs and disagreements between members that can be used to deal with issues arising. Just as genograms can show the assets and spiritual interactions across generations, Hodge (2005) also demonstrates how an ecomap can demonstrate spiritual support and connections between people. It must be remembered, however, that just as constructing an ecomap can foster positive debate and discussion it may give rise to matters that evoke strong feeling and conflict between family members. You need to be aware of this when working with families in this way and consider ways in which you may lessen tension arising from disagreements whilst acknowledging the value of each person's contribution and understanding. Setting some ground rules first may help. Acknowledge that there may be disagreements and state that this is healthy and should be allowed. By making people aware of possible differences and encouraging participants to discuss them you may find a greater willingness to explore issues in more depth.

How to construct an ecomap

Ecomaps are fairly easy to construct. On a large sheet of paper draw a circle in the middle and place the family or individual member's name within it. Following this, a series of smaller circles can be placed around this circle. In each of these place the name of the organisation, institution, social group, family or individual with which the family has connections. The nature of the relationship between the individual and 'circle' can be made clear by the line linking the two. Thick lines indicate strong connections, broken lines indicate weak connections and wavy or crossed lines indicate stress associated with the connection. The following ecomap concerning Mark provides an example.

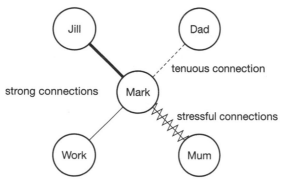

Mark's relationships

The ecomap is valuable because of its direct and immediate visual impact. A wealth of information is presented concerning relationships and perceptions of these. Whilst it was originally developed as a tool to aid social workers' and family therapists' assessments of family situations it has, as noted above, value in creating a working partnership in which the service user takes an active role in the assessment. The result of this has been that shared insight has aided planning and subsequent interventions are located firmly within the living-space of the service user. The first composition may help the initial assessment but, as we know, human life is never static and changes occur continually. Therefore, constructing further ecomaps at various points throughout the interventive phase can help social workers and service users to evaluate outcomes together. It can also identify possible sources of support to assist the family or individual in working towards change. It is important to note, however, that an ecomap leaves out certain information. For instance, in the above, we are not told Mark's age, where he lives or anything about his family history or life experience. These are questions that can be asked during the construction of the ecomap. However, by combining the ecomap with the genogram we begin to get a more rounded picture of an individual's or family's life and relationships. Hartman (1995) describes the development, construction and uses of ecomaps in social work settings.

It is important to gain an understanding of some of the possible implications and impacts of the models and tools used to make an assessment. This helps us to tailor the tools to particular circumstances and to ensure that issues arising form the process are effectively dealt with. The following activity gives you an opportunity to compile your own ecomap.

ACTIVITY 2.2

Take a piece of flip chart paper and place your name in a circle at the centre of it. Draw circles around the outside of your circle and place the names of family, friends, acquaintances and clubs or organisations with whom you are involved. In this way you will begin to construct your own map. Consider carefully the relationships and connections you have with the various organisations, agencies, groups, families and individuals that you have placed in the outer circles. By using a combination of different lines, thicknesses and comments show the strength of these relationships and your feelings towards them. You may be able to compile a retrospective ecomap that may help, in some way, to demonstrate changes that have occurred throughout your life. Of course, when drawing such ecomaps retrospectively you are open to interpreting the past in the light of the present. However, for experiential purposes it forms a useful exercise. Keep your ecomap for later consultation and adaptation if you wish. It may be useful to compare the ecomap with your genogram and to see how they fit together, what different information each map includes and what each says about you. Ask yourself how these tools might add to an effective assessment when working as a social worker.

The genogram was extremely useful in the case study of Mrs Jones and her concerns with regard to Damien. The case study continues below to demonstrate what additional information could be gained from an ecomap.

CASE STUDY

At a later assessment session it was agreed to construct an ecomap (see overleaf). The intention was to find out exactly what levels of support Mrs Jones now had, how she felt about the support and how this compared with the support she had enjoyed previously. It was also thought likely that in the compilation of the ecomap it may be that further sources of support would be discussed, identified and an interventive strategy determined.

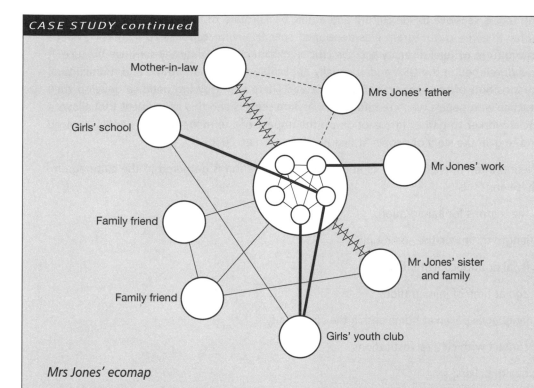

Mrs Jones' ecomap

It quickly became apparent that Mr and Mrs Jones had mutual friends, Mr Jones worked and enjoyed this, and the girls enjoyed good relations with their school and youth club. Mrs Jones, however, had little if anything to occupy herself outside of the family unit. In fact, since the deterioration in her relationship with her mother in law she had little support within the family. Her father had not seen her for some years. She described her relationship with him as stormy in the past. On further exploration it seemed that they disagreed on most things since the death of her mother. This culminated in her marriage two years after to Mr Jones. They had been seeing one another for some time but Mrs Jones' father had never approved of the relationship. When she married Mr Jones her father visited only rarely until he ceased visiting at all some years ago. A source of support and friendship in Mr Jones' sister had been lost after an argument following the death of Mr Jones' father.

The ecomap proved extremely useful in presenting a visual and pictorial display of relationships and isolation. It gave rise, also, to the beginning formulation of an interventive strategy aimed at securing positive and supportive connections for Mrs Jones outside of the family environment and within her control.

Culturagrams

A relatively new assessment tool that is similar to the ecomap and genogram has recently added to the social work repertoire: that of the culturagram. As the name suggests it is designed to assist social workers in the analysis of the meaning and impact of culture in the life of those families and individuals being assessed. This is an important tool in developing a culturally sensitive approach to social work. Service users are acknowledged as being the experts on their own lives and situations rather than social workers assuming that they know best.

The tool is sensitive to the culture and ethnic background of individuals. Congress (1994) states that the culturagram was developed specifically in response to increasing needs arising from cultural diversity and the crucial importance of ethnically-sensitive practice. It was developed in the USA and is equally applicable to the multiethnic and multicultural composition of contemporary British society. There is a growing need to develop such practice with people who are refugees or asylum seekers and this assessment tool allows a social worker to gather information on the impact of the move for individuals involved and to gain the story of people at first hand (see Parker, 2000).

There are ten important factors about which information is gathered in the culturagram. These are:

- the reasons for immigration;

- length of time in the community;

- legal or undocumented status;

- age at time of immigration;

- language spoken at home and in the community;

- contact with cultural institutions;

- health beliefs;

- holidays and special events;

- the impact of crisis and significant events;

- values held about family, education and work.

Constructing a culturagram involves a skilled use of communication skills. Asking sensitive questions is not easy in any situation. Where people may be suspicious of authority figures asking questions, sometimes because of particularly traumatic past experiences, great sensitivity is required. Social workers must explain very clearly why such information is needed, what it will be used for and who will have access to it. This may slow the process of assessment but it is important if the information is going to be used in the most effective ways. Rushing or pushing too hard may result in spurious information being given or may indeed impede the development of constructive working relationships. Sometimes working at the pace of service users will involve you developing and using skills of assertion within social work teams, especially when you are being pressed to achieve objectives and targets within specified timeframes.

It is also important to be mindful of language and communication issues, especially where English is a second language. Social workers will need to ask careful, concrete questions and be prepared to repeat or put certain questions to one side. Summaries of discussion, paraphrasing and sharing written copies of the information can help in developing good practice. The information gathered in response to the ten areas highlighted above is drawn together to form a culturagram in a diagram similar to the ecomap (see overleaf).

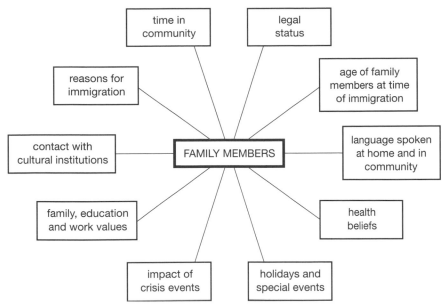

Culturagrams

The use of the culturagram is important to the social worker in demonstrating the significant differences raised between family members that may have an impact on acculturation – how individuals begin to fit in to a new culture – and family functioning. The diversity of beliefs among family members may become very clear. This knowledge can be used to understand and reconcile differences between family members.

Congress (1994) believes that the use of the culturagram may empower family members by helping them to see their cultural background as important and may point to areas within the family and to external social institutions that need social work involvement and support. The following case study exemplifies some of the uses such an assessment may have.

CASE STUDY

Baljinder was 18 years old and was hoping to study law at university in the coming year. She had been asked by her mother to visit her uncle and brothers in a small village in Bangladesh in the summer before going to university. Baljinder was nervous about this request and although her mother had promised her that it was just a visit, she did not wish to go. This nervousness stemmed from the experience a friend of hers had the previous summer. Baljinder's friend had been forced into marriage, escaping later in the year, returning to England and now having few friends within her family or community. Baljinder's mother promised her that during her visit she would not ask her to marry against her will. A social worker from the local area working specifically with the Bangladeshi community assisted Baljinder and her mother to work through these anxieties. By compiling a culturagram, Baljinder was able to see the process of her family moving to England, the importance of consultation within her family and the strong Islamic faith that guided family decisions. As a result of this, Baljinder was convinced that her mother was indeed proposing a family trip and was able to go and enjoy this summer prior to university.

As Congress (1994) states:

The culturagram is a powerful tool for helping social workers assess and intervene appropriately with culturally diverse families. It is rooted in a model of cultural pluralism which stresses the intrinsic value of culturally diverse families pursuing their own styles, customs, values and language while recognising that different degrees of acculturation do occur...
(Congress, 1994, page 538)

This case example demonstrates how culturagrams can identify changing attitudes and influences of culture between generations.

Baljinder's mother was pleased that her daughter could see that she would not be forced into marriage. The move to England in the 1970s to gain work and support her husband's mother and father back in Bangladesh was significant to her. Completing the culturagram allowed her to see the changes in attitudes between her and her daughter's generation. The expectation that she would move and that her husband would support his parents was never questioned at the time. Whilst she would not have changed her move to England or the reasons for it she was convinced that her desire to support her daughter in what she wanted came in part from her own experiences. It was the completion of the culturagram that helped her to understand this.

It must be remembered that events do not always work out so well. Compiling a culturagram can raise conflicts and tensions within families. It is important that social workers do not fall into the trap of working through conflicts in a way that reflects their own cultural values and position but to work at the pace of service users and show respect for their value systems.

Culturagrams in working with abuse

Culturagrams have been employed in the sensitive area of elder abuse and domestic violence (Brownell, 1997). It is possible to use a culturagram as a screening instrument to assess and detect abuse and to promote culturally sensitive practice. Brownell (1997) suggests that it is an adjunct to professional assessment that allows the social worker to gain a clearer understanding of cultural values, belief systems and experiences and so to intervene more effectively in a person-centred way rather than one based on an appreciation of one's own values. She reports on a number of case examples including the Chinese American community, the Polish community, Latin American and Indian/South Asian communities. The culturagram helped to identify particular aspects of culture and values that were important in planning further work and developing culturally sensitive approaches to practice. What must be remembered, of course, is that this tool was developed in the US context and may need some adaptation for use in the UK.

Often, our own culture becomes taken for granted because we live within it and repro-duce it from day to day. In this activity you are asked to compile your own culturagram and to examine how this tool can bring to the fore aspects of your life and culture that were perhaps buried beneath the surface or taken for granted.

Using the areas identified in the diagram above, construct a culturagram for your family. Pick out key points and issues. It may be that you have not moved country but perhaps moved town or county. This too can demonstrate cultural issues that are important to the way you see the world and respond to it. For instance, the terms we use for the meals we eat differ across different parts of the UK. Other aspects of language may be specific to a region. These all help to identify us and can lead to assumptions being made about who we are. By identifying our own cultural values we can begin to recognise the importance of everyday rituals in others.

Flow diagrams and life road maps

The previous assessment tools can provide a wealth of information concerning the ecolog-ical location of the individual and family, family histories, patterns and norms. The flow diagram and the life road map stand at a mid-point between the person's living system and the patterns and norms that develop within families. They can be used to provide a chronological history of significant events and moves in the family's and/or individuals' lives. These tools also serve to locate the person in space and time in the present; giving a snapshot look at how the individual came to be where they are and what experiences have had an impact in making them so. Like the genogram, flow diagrams and life road maps can demonstrate the various routes a person has taken to where they are today, and like the ecomap they firmly locate the person or family unit in a specific context in place and history. It demonstrates matters of importance to individual service users.

The number of movements that a family or individual has in a given space of time may be of great significance to understanding the particular situation for which they are now seeking help from a social worker. This information may also identify patterns and events that were not consciously considered by service users. One interactive way of charting movements that can be employed with adults and equally so with children is the construction of a flow diagram. Starting from birth or, indeed, some other specified and agreed point, the individual or family is asked to complete a box for every place where they have lived. It is important to include dates as the length of time spent in places can be of the utmost significance. If possible, it is useful to provide information of the family composition at these various stages to consider the various expected and unexpected transitions that the family may have undergone. In this way, the compilation of a flow diagram can be undertaken alongside the construction of a genogram. The boxes of the flow diagram are connected to one another until the present in terms of time and location is reached (see flow diagram, p.56).

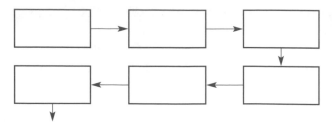

Flow diagrams

Again, like genograms, ecomaps and culturagrams, the flow diagram has a great potential for visual impact. It can locate times of turbulence and upset, times of change, consistencies and inconsistencies in a family's pattern of life. This can have an immediate impact on service users when completing the flow diagram. They may be encouraged, by seeing the results of their diagram, to express a range of issues and concerns connected with these moves and their own histories. The patterns that emerge can help explain how and why the person is located where they are today. At the very least, the flow diagram allows for the formation and further exploration of hypotheses. As such it is a valuable assessment tool in the social worker's repertoire.

ACTIVITY **2.4**

Take a large piece of paper and draw as many boxes as you think you might need to detail your moves. Complete a flow diagram representing all the house moves you have experienced by filling in the date and place of move in each of the boxes. Wherever possible add information that you remember from the move. For instance, who was with you when you moved and did anyone stay behind? You might have moved because of your parents' jobs, or perhaps moved into a place of your own for the first time. What roles did each person involved in the move have? This could relate to a parental role, a partner or child amongst others.

Try to think about the experiences associated with these moves and the people who were involved, what changes there have been in your family or living group composition and your associated feelings. Again, this activity can evoke strong feelings and reactions. These may appear when using such techniques with service users, and being aware of this yourself is good preparation for an understanding and sensitive response.

Repeat this activity for someone you have worked with or someone you know well from your past. (Remember to ensure the anonymity of the person.) Does the diagram assist in your understanding of their present situation? It may bring to light points for further exploration. For instance, a reasonable hypothesis to make about a homesick person who has experienced very few moves during their life but has just begun a university course away from home may be that the homesickness is connected. Of course, this need not necessarily be the case and you would need to ask further questions to check this idea, but seeing the pattern can help you forge these questions.

What information did completion of this activity provide you with that you were not aware of before this activity? You may have found out something about your own life and moves or those of the other person you have considered. Think about the possible ways in which the completion of a life road map may help you in formulating questions to extend the depth of an assessment.

We can see how the use of a flow diagram assisted in the continuing assessment of the Jones family case study.

A flow diagram (see below) was undertaken with Mrs Jones and her present family. This indicated that in the two years prior to the death of her mother she had moved frequently, living in a variety of locations in the country. It was at this time that she met her present husband and began to lose more contact with her father. She expressed a belief that her father blamed her for not being with her mother during her last two years of life. This seemed to have some substance but more importantly it brought up an issue warranting further exploration.

There was a further period of frequent moves that seemed to the social worker to have significance. In the year immediately after the death of Mr Jones' father and the birth of Damien the family moved three times because of Mr Jones' job. Since that time, however, they have settled in one place.

The information collected provided the social worker with areas to explore further. It gave Mrs Jones a level of insight and understanding into her life that she had not had before and the process helped establish a working relationship between her and the social worker.

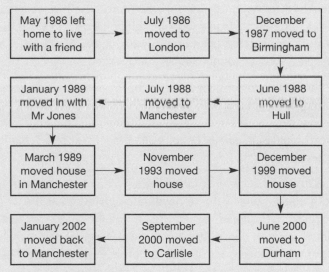

Mrs Jones' flow diagram of moves

Two significant points were raised by this exercise. First, it was apparent that Mrs Jones' stormy relationship with her father and disagreements with him were long lived, and, in fact, began some time before the death of her mother and before she met and began living with Mr Jones. Also, it seemed potentially significant that there were so many moves in the year following Mr Jones' father's death. This provided opportunities for further discussion and exploration. Prior to such a focused consideration of her life's events and chronology Mrs Jones did not realise the potential significance of these. As she said I was so wrapped up in the events themselves that I paid little attention to the details.

Using road maps

Chronicling the number and dates of moves, and gathering information concerning family patterns, changes and norms by the completion of a genogram, provides useful data for the analysis of families and from which to begin to develop interventions. However, it is not only moves and family compositions, histories and transitions that are perceived as significant by people. To gain a more comprehensive picture of the situation, the social worker may compile a 'life road map' with the service user.

A life road map is a pictorial representation of the major events and occurrences, rather than just moves, in the life of the service user. It portrays these events as perceived by service users. This can be valuable in keeping a person's attention and may seem a little more exciting than a simple flow diagram. Undertaking a life road map, therefore, validates the perceptions of service users who decide on the importance of events to include. This demonstrates respect for their self-worth and their active participation in the process of assessment and intervention. It is helpful for social workers to remember at all times during the assessment process that service users are expert on their own lives and experiences.

Originally, the life road map was developed as a technique for use with children in care settings, and especially those engaged in the process of life story work prior to placement in substitute families. It is still important in completing this crucial work with children who have been in the looked after system and social workers can use this technique effectively, as with other tools, to establish positive working relationships. However, the use of life road maps can be much wider. It has been used successfully with a range of service users, adults and older people as well as young people and children.

It is useful to take a little time to consider some of the ways the use of life road maps can contribute to the compilation of a life story book. For instance, can you think of possible dangers and limitations in using this technique? Are there likely to be differences between completing a life road map as an adolescent or as an older adult other than the length of time that can be covered?

It is clear that focusing on major events in a person's life will provide rich material that forms the backcloth against which that individual may view their life. It can form an immediate visual display that can itself be included in the life story book and can identify events to be explored in more depth. It may be, however, that the activity raises very painful memories and social workers must be aware of the need for sensitivity and be able to work with distress. It may also be the case that some aspects of a person's life have been forgotten or mistaken and it is again important that people feel comfortable enough to leave out areas of their lives. This may present some differences depending on the age and developmental stage of the individual completing the life road map.

A life road map is fairly simple to construct (see p.59). The social worker asks the service user to draw a 'road' on a large piece of paper. The road will have a number of bends and turns in it. The social worker then asks the service user to write a brief comment about an event in their life that they themselves perceive as significant at each turn and twist in the road. As events are being written on to the road, the social worker and service user may talk about them and weigh up together the significance of each. This will help to identify further areas for exploration and clarify other points.

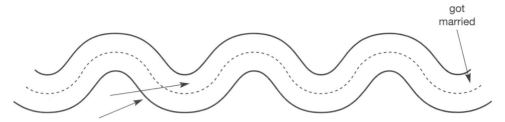

got
married

Insert perceived significant events where the road turns

A life road map

It is not strictly necessary that events are written in chronological order but the idea of a road may lend itself to this. When seen as part of a larger assessment, it may be more useful to link data from each session and activity. If this were to be the case then a chronological account would be preferable. However, it is, in the end, the information gathered for the assessment that is of paramount importance whatever service user group you are working with, or whatever the purpose of your assessment. In this instance the information relates to the perceptions of the service user and tells you something about their construction of the world, how they perceive it working and how they themselves interact with it. This material can be used, again, to stimulate conversation and analysis of issues, to gain insight for the service user and to prepare the ground for intervention. Bear in mind the following questions when completing a life road map with service users.

• What is it that service users want to change?

• What is of concern to social welfare institutions?

• Is there anything within the assessment we can use as a basis for, or to measure change?

ACTIVITY 2.5

Again, it will be useful to your development and for your understanding of the process of undertaking an assessment using these techniques for you to compile a life road map representing some of the significant events that you have experienced. Remember the 'significance' is based upon your perception of events and not what you think might be considered significant by others. Try to think about the experiences associated with these experiences and the people, times and settings involved. If you need to use more than one piece of paper to complete your map this is all right. It can provide a useful learning experience for applying the technique later with service users.

How might you employ this technique in a practice situation?

You would need to be prepared with paper, pens and perhaps some ideas for starting the map. Depending on the age and understanding of the person involved, you could use the time drawing the 'road' to build a relationship and to put the individual at ease. With an older person the process could take a more matter of fact approach. As with all techniques, a clear explanation of the task and its purpose is essential.

List some of the ways a life road map may help in identifying areas to work upon following the assessment.

You might include the identification of strengths, individuals important to the person completing the map or specific events that have occurred in the life of that individual in your list.

In our continuing case study we see how Mrs Jones used the life road map to explore events and issues in her life.

CASE STUDY

In order to complement and add to the data collected from Mrs Jones and her family she completed a life road map with the social worker (see below). This brought to the fore a number of issues not previously mentioned. The genogram presented her family history as reasonably stable. However, when completing the life road map it was clear that a significant event for Mrs Jones was that her father left her mother for a period of a year when she was 11. Not surprisingly, her illness during the pregnancy with Damien figured highly in her perceptions of significant events. Apart from this little other data emerged. However, even the incidental material has value; it demonstrates the feelings invested in certain things and events add to the overall picture of the subject of the assessment.

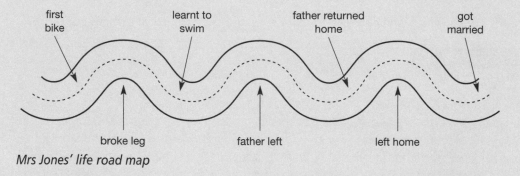

Mrs Jones' life road map

This conflated view of part of the life road map drawn by Mrs Jones demonstrates some of the important events that help the social worker make sense of who she is and what is important to her. The map is interesting. Mrs Jones included the positively perceived aspects of her life towards the top of the map and the negative ones towards the bottom. Whilst too much significance can be read into this, life roads maps can be used in ways to discuss the significance of events and the value attached to them.

C H A P T E R   S U M M A R Y

Assessment is a skilled professional process. The collection of information is integral to the completion of an effective assessment. The manner of the assessment and the methods employed to gather information, to synthesise it and to begin to form hypotheses for further exploration are all important factors to take into account. This is recognised in the educational requirements for social work. Models and tools must be chosen with sensitivity and with a clear purpose in mind. It is useful to bear in mind the following questions:

- How can I involve those people who are the focus of the assessment?

- Why do you want to collect this information?

- For what purpose(s) will it be used?

- Who will see the information?

The five tools we have discussed in this chapter help to structure the process of assessment. Not only do they provide an interactive and participative way of collecting information but they also elicit important topics to explore further and to determine the focus of future assessment. Using these tools can also provide key insights for service users completing them. Although insight into one's situation is unlikely to promote change in itself, it can encourage motivation to work towards change and by doing so assist in planning and implementing effective implementation strategies.

These tools and techniques form a useful adjunct to the use of interpersonal or communication skills, such as exploration, questioning and probing. It must be remembered that they form part of an overall and comprehensive approach to assessment that will also take into account case files, reports, third party statements, verbal and written communications from others involved, and full and candid discussion with the subjects of the assessment.

It is imperative that social work is seen to be a discipline that is effective. It should do what it claims to be able to do (whilst allowing for human changeability). Essential to this is promoting a model of practice that is research-minded and that evaluates the effects of its interventions. The use of these techniques to collect data at a cross-section in the life of the family or member of that unit enables the social worker and the subject to monitor change in some small way. This is integral to the development of good social work practice but further research into the efficacy of these models is also needed.

Assessment is and should be purposeful as we saw in Chapter 1. It is undertaken in order to determine targets and goals for change to improve the quality of life of those involved. The tools introduced here are important in providing data to enable the planning and implementation of social work interventions designed to achieve desired and agreed change. We saw the tools being used with Mrs Jones and her family. A genogram assisted in beginning to compile information about the family's history and highlighted other information that may have been important, especially Mrs Jones' relationship with her mother-in-law. In later sessions an ecomap was used to look at support and other family relationships and the completion of a flow diagram and life road map highlighted other significant aspects of her life. All the activities undertaken helped the worker to engage with Mrs Jones and her family, to encourage participation in the assessment and to begin to focus on areas of concern and issues that could become targets and goals for intervention. They provided also a baseline from which change could be measured. This could not be done in a rigorous scientific and quantitative way. However, qualitative change could be measured and alterations to her and her family's life space, patterns and development could be explored, discussed and promoted.

Before we turn in the next chapter to a discussion of how we use our assessments to plan for effective practice with service users and carers consider the following activity.

ACTIVITY *2.6*

Read through the case study material relating to Rebecca, Melissa and Irene or Gladys Beaumont that you were introduced to in Chapter 1. Using your knowledge of the tools for assessment discussed in this chapter, compile a genogram, ecomap, culturagram, flow diagram or life road map for these service users as far as you are able.

This activity will help to consolidate this knowledge. We have not provided examples of what you may have found here as this gives you an opportunity to check through your understanding of this chapter and the models employed. You do need, however, to bear in mind the following questions:

- *What further information do you think you might need or wish to explore?*

- *How might you get this information?*

- *How would you seek to involve the service users as fully as possible in collecting this information?*

FURTHER
READING

Barker, P (1986) Basic family therapy. Oxford: Blackwell.

Whilst this text discusses the principles of family therapy, it is useful for social workers because of its treatment of diagrammatic tools for assessment.

McGoldrick, M, Gerson, R and Shellenberger, S (1999) Genograms: assessment and intervention. 2nd edition. New York: Norton.

This book represents an essential text for those social workers and students who want to expand their knowledge of and improve their practice in the use of genograms for assessment.

Chapter 3

Developing, making and writing plans for effective social work

Introduction

Assessment, as we noted in the previous two chapters, is the keystone holding together effective social work practice. Whilst the recommendations of the inquiry into the death of Victoria Climbié emphasise the importance of assessment, they also highlight the importance of subsequent planning and the need to include and consult with the child and carers in developing action plans (recommendation 25). Once information is gathered and an ongoing engagement with service users established it is important to make plans to determine what can be done, how it can be done and who will do what. In this chapter you will be introduced to the development of plans in social work based on assessments and will explore key issues arising in respect of ethics, power, professionalism in social work and anti-oppressive practice. In making plans, you will be asked to consider the effects of working with other professions and with informal carers and service users.

Students will be invited to consider how a plan is made in child and family work and work with adults. Contemporary guidance and advice on care planning will be provided and activities will help students to make links between knowledge and practice throughout this chapter. A critique of the language of 'care plans' and the importance for students to be aware of the centrality of service user involvement will permeate the discussion. A particular focus will concern the writing of care or service delivery plans and the importance of accessibility and involvement to make plans effective will be emphasised through student centred activities. Students will question the purpose and use of plans, how they can be person-focused and proactive in achieving agreed aims and in charting a course for intervention.

What is a plan?

Perhaps the immediate thing that comes to mind when thinking about plans is the scale drawing made when building a house or extension. These plans provide details of what would have to take place to reach the desired outcome – building the house or extension. They provide a visual map of the elements making up the plan and a view of what that outcome would look like. This is a useful analogy for considering social work plans. They are 'maps' based on prior and ongoing negotiations with those involved. A social work plan, however, is wider still. It presents a detailed picture of a situation, those involved and what action might be taken, and by whom these actions might be taken in order to meet assessed or identified needs.

One useful element that can be taken from plans for a building is the notion of 'planning permission'. The negotiation of a plan with those who would be involved from a professional angle is clear. If services and agencies cannot contribute in the ways you have identified, the plan is unlikely to be effective. Also, if the service user is not involved in the negotiation and agreement of the plan then plans may either ignore and contravene the rights of the service user or be doomed to failure. So plans like assessment must be built on a developing relationship between you as a social worker, the other agencies and professionals who might be contributing to the plan and service users. It is important that an ethical approach be taken from the outset. Not only is this part of the National Occupational Standards but it is central to the Code of Practice for employees and is enshrined in the legislation and guidance concerning the development of plans.

To help you think about the process of planning and to consider what negotiations, agreements and actions might be involved try the following activity.

ACTIVITY **3.1**

Think back to the time you decided to study to become a social worker. Write down how you came to that decision. Who did you talk to when making your decision? What plans did you have to make? For instance, did you have to plan moving house or area, did you have to examine how you might manage financially, and were there any family or relationship considerations that needed taking into account before deciding where you might apply, what type of programme you would study and who would be central in helping you achieve your goals?

You may have written how the first rush of enthusiasm to study was tempered by the practical and emotional considerations that arose when planning how to achieve your aims. You may have needed to speak with parents, partners or children and to come to some understanding with people close to you. You may have had to consider the financial implications of studying. Would the bursary be enough to help you study? Are there other financial commitments that need to be dealt with? You may also have had to plan with others to take on roles and responsibilities that you have assumed but would not be able to continue to do whilst studying. The range of matters to think about mirror many of those that occur when negotiating social work plans with service users and with other professionals. It is important, therefore, that you understand some of the complex issues raised when making plans.

SMART planning

A useful way of remembering the core elements involved in planning can be found in the mnemonic SMART which relates to the following:

Specific in respect of aims and objectives of the plan and the roles or tasks undertaken by those involved.

Measurable in terms of the outcomes and goals that are agreed upon.

Achievable goals and outcomes so that those involved are likely to succeed and enhance their motivation for change.

Realistic and relevant outcomes that maintain a focus on the core issues identified by those involved.

Timely and **t**ime-limited in addressing current issues and setting in train a plan that has a review point not too distant in the future.

Plans for children in need

The *Every Child Matters* agenda and the Children Act 2004 have led to a joint planning and commissioning framework for Children's Trusts that considers the planning and provision of children's services as a whole in a local area. The emphasis in planning services is focused on and attempts to involve those using services, based on local needs assessment and agreed by a range of stakeholders integral to the process. Planning at this level aims to be preventive. The Department of Health, Department for Education and Employment, Home Office (2000) is clear that plans for working with children in need are central to measuring the success of any subsequent work that is undertaken. If they are to be used as a measure they need to be both clear and feasible. It is the assessment and analysis of this that forms the basis of the plan which will be attuned to the specific needs and circumstances of the child and family in question. The plan will also differ according to the reasons for undertaking an assessment. The following box shows some of the different plans identified by the Department of Health, all of which have accompanying guidance linked to them.

> ### Types of Social Work Plans for Children in Need, following Department of Health, Department for Education and Employment, Home Office (2000)
>
> **Children in Need Plan** *Negotiated with child, family and contributing agencies (see Department of Health and Cleaver, 2000).*
>
> **Child Protection Plan** *After a child protection case conference and assessment under s. 47 of the Children Act.*
>
> **Care Plan for Looked After Children.**
>
> **Care Plans** *For a child who is the subject of a supervision or care order or for whom adoption is planned.*
>
> **Pathway Plan** *For a young person in care or leaving care.*

The general principles outlined for making plans with children and families include the importance of negotiations and agreement, where possible, with the child or young person and key family members. Also, the objectives agreed should be reasonable and achievable and sufficient time should be allowed to achieve these outcomes as suggested by SMART planning. The question of resources and appropriate services is important. A plan will be unlikely to succeed if it needs particular resources that are in short supply or difficult to obtain. A further central concern is that, whilst it is important to take into account everyone's views, the child or young person must be the focus of the plan. Practice guidance from the Department of Health and Social Services Inspectorate (1995) and repeated in the *Framework for the assessment of children in need and their families* (Department of Health, Department for Education and Employment, Home Office, 2000) outlines the following elements to be included in plans:

- the objectives of the plan;

- what services will be provided and by whom;

- timing and nature of contact between professionals and families;

- the purpose of services and contact;

- the commitments to be met by the family;

- the commitments to be met by professionals, including attending to matters of diversity and equal opportunities;

- specification of those parts of the plan which can be renegotiated and those which cannot;

- what needs to change and what goals need to be achieved;

- what is unacceptable care;

- what sanctions will be used if the child is placed in danger;

- what preparation and support children and adults will receive if they appear in court as a witness in criminal proceedings.

Plans are part of the overall social work process as noted earlier and as stated in the following quotation:

> It is essential that the plan is constructed on the basis of the findings from the assessment and that this plan is reviewed and refined over time to ensure the agreed case objectives are achieved. Specific outcomes for the child, expressed in terms of their health and development can be measured. These provide objective evidence against which to evaluate whether the child and family have been provided with appropriate services and ultimately the child's wellbeing is optimal.
> (Department of Health, Department for Education and Employment, Home Office, 2000, 4.37)

A plan made to assist a child in need should have a statement recording the timing for its review and how this will take place. Regular review is counted as good practice. The processes of review will be considered in Chapter 5. Before we return to the case of Rebecca and Melissa, it might be helpful to consider the following plan in respect of another service user, Peter.

CASE STUDY

Peter was 10 years old. He had recently been diagnosed as having attention deficit hyperactivity disorder (ADHD), a condition that meant he had considerable difficulty staying focused and a tendency to become very angry about seemingly minor things in a short space of time. He was not able to control his anger and was often physically violent to his mother and broke his toys, glasses and pots in the house. He had recently been excluded from school for hitting a teacher in one of his outbursts.

With the agreement of his mother, the school had contacted the local social work team. A case discussion including Peter himself, his teachers, an educational psychologist, general practitioner, his mother and a social worker had been called following an initial assessment of his situation. A plan to return and support him at school was developed. The plan was written and recorded as a form of agreement. This plan, which was made accessible to Peter as the focus of the work, follows.

Care plan for Peter
Aims and objectives
The aim of this plan is to set out the ways in which Peter can return to school and learn to control his behaviour.

By each person agreeing to the actions set out in the plan Peter will be able to return to school and be supported in controlling his behaviour.

Who will do what
After this meeting Peter will attend an appointment with Dr R, (GP) who will discuss possible medicine with Peter and his mother.

Mum and Mrs B (teacher) will meet with Dr G, educational psychologist, who will discuss ways of managing his behaviour in the classroom, consider any special needs and requirements to maintain him at school.

67

CASE STUDY *continued*

Peter will attend meetings as arranged and will work with everyone trying to help him control his temper.

Susan F (social worker) will discuss with Peter and mum ways of managing his behaviour at home, reducing the number of times Peter gets angry and hits out.

When we will meet
Susan will visit mum and Peter at home after school on Thursday evenings. Susan will visit weekly for the first four weeks of this agreement and a fortnight after this before the first review.

What are we meeting to do?
When we meet we will discuss how things have changed, what we want to achieve and look at ways in which Peter can recognise when he is about to become cross, what happens inside when he gets cross and what he might do instead of hitting out or breaking things.

Susan, Mrs B, Peter and his mother will work out a plan to reintroduce Peter into school over a period of four weeks. Mrs B will be informed about the ways Peter might control his temper and will make this possible within school.

What we expect
Everyone involved in this plan can expect to be listened to and taken seriously. We will all attend meetings arranged promptly and if, for any reasons, someone cannot attend an arranged meeting, this should be discussed with all involved as soon as possible.

Review and renegotiation
This agreement will be reviewed by a meeting of all people involved in six weeks time.

If there is a need to get together prior to this then a review can be asked for by any person involved in this agreement by asking the social worker.

ACTIVITY **3.2**

In Chapter 1 you were introduced to Rebecca, her mother, Melissa and grandmother, Irene. An initial assessment, using the CAF and the assessment triangle from the Framework, was carried out and recommendations were agreed:

- *to undertake family work with Melissa and Irene;*
- *for Irene to take Rebecca twice each week and offer Melissa a break;*
- *for Melissa to attend a young mothers' group to gain support and advice.*

This initial assessment saw the first stages of planning. Indeed, without prior planning the assessment would have been unfocused and unlikely to be effective in considering Rebecca's needs. However, the development of plans for social work intervention takes place in earnest following the completion of an initial assessment. Your task as a social worker now concerns the discussion and negotiations necessary, assuming you have

ACTIVITY 3.2 continued

the agreement of your team leader, service users and carers, with the services who will carry out this work. In this particular case, you may look at a 'continuing care' of 'family support team' within the local authority or in a voluntary agency with which the authority has a service agreement. Such teams have different names, and indeed, different functions in different areas. Considering the above recommendations, begin to draw together a plan for Rebecca using the elements outlined above.

You may have produced something akin to the following plan. However, note where there are similarities and where there are differences between your plan and the one outlined and consider why these might have occurred and what they might mean for the people involved.

CASE STUDY

Care plan for Rebecca Krajic
Aims and objectives
This care plan aims to:

- *provide Melissa with a break from caring for Rebecca;*

- *provide Melissa an opportunity to gain support and advice from other young mothers;*

- *work towards improving the relationship between Melissa and Irene.*

The objective of the plan is to offer the best possible start in life for Rebecca.

Services
A member of Southside Family Support Team will work with Irene and Melissa to identify causes of friction and to find ways in which they can reduce tension and support each other in caring for Rebecca.

June Bridge, health visitor, will secure a place and introduce Melissa into the young mum's support group.

What will happen
The social worker will meet with Irene and Melissa at the Family Support Team office for one hour for the next four weeks. Childcare support will be arranged for Rebecca within the team for the duration of these sessions.

These meetings will be used:

- *to explore the family history and relationship between Irene and Melissa;*

- *identify tensions and strengths in their relationship;*

- *seek alternative ways of negotiating and behaving towards each other;*

- *to develop an agreement to work together for Rebecca;*

- *to negotiate the best times to create a regular slot for Irene to look after Rebecca.*

What we all expect

It is expected that Melissa and Irene will attend each session promptly, informing the social worker as soon as possible if it is not possible to attend.

The social worker will attend each session promptly and will inform both Melissa and Irene if it is not possible to attend.

If any session is missed, this will be rearranged as soon as possible.

The social worker will ensure that childcare is provided for Rebecca during these sessions.

Melissa will attend the young mums' support group regularly.

Melissa will ensure that Rebecca has clean nappies, clothing and a bottle when she attends the family support sessions and the support group.

The social worker will help Irene and Melissa agree the best times for Irene to look after Rebecca.

Renegotiation and review

This plan will be reviewed by everyone involved after the four sessions have taken place at the family support team.

If anything happens that may affect this plan, this can be discussed at the following session or, if necessary, by contacting the social worker, Melissa or Irene between sessions.

Any changes or amendments to the plan should be agreed by all involved if at all possible.

Outcomes

At the end of the four sessions we will review how Melissa and Irene feel about their relationship and where to proceed from here. We will discuss whether arrangements for providing Melissa a break from Rebecca are working. We will review Melissa's attendance at the young mums' support group.

Care plans are central to building on assessments and producing an effective map for the intervention to proceed. Care plans are not, however, the property and preserve of the social worker and, to work best on behalf of your service users, they must be negotiated and jointly agreed. Of course, as we have seen, plans will need to include some aspects of social work that are not open for negotiation. These need to be clearly explained. Indeed, when social workers are honest and open about sensitive, difficult and non-negotiable areas of practice, service users are able to appreciate this. What is not acceptable is keeping hidden any sanction or aspect of the plan that might have to be used under certain circumstances. For instance, it is important to qualify issues of confidentiality. A service user might want to be assured that whatever they say will be treated as confidential to the session. This is not always possible. A service user who talks about their own experiences of child abuse when the abuser still has contact with and access to other children will not be able to have that information kept confidential. This kind of situation can be spelt out clearly in agreed plans. SMART planning can assist in dealing with some of these issues, such as keeping a focus on relevant issues that can be achieved ethically, legally and practically in the time-scales allowed. Using such a mnemonic as a set of guiding principles with people using services can assist and enhance their involvement.

An effective plan is a blueprint for action that looks two ways. It is retrospective looking towards the assessment, whilst recognising that an assessment should also be an ongoing process, and it is prospective in looking forward to working with service users to effect change (see illustration below).

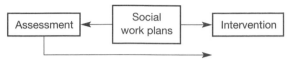

Plans as retrospective and prospective

We will now explore the use and development of care plans in care management practice with adult service users.

Planning in care management and adult services

Making, developing and writing plans for adult service users within care management is known as care planning. This process is also one of the hallmarks of the SAP and is described here by Jacqui Smith, the Minister for Health:

> *Once assessments have taken place, older people will then receive their own individual care plan. The plan will clearly explain the detail of the help that will be available and also what should happen in the event of an emergency or if circumstances change.* (Department of Health press release, 16 August 2001).

User empowerment, equal opportunities and the care plan

Care planning has always been an element of social work with adults, but never more so than within the context of care management. It is the dynamic process which follows the assessment of need and the vehicle for achieving the desired and agreed outcomes. In the shaping of care plans within care management, early guidance (SSI, Department of Health, 1991a) drew on theories of user empowerment as the guiding principles on which practice was to be based. The service user and carer were to be at the heart of the process; it was their preferences and genuine choice that should steer how the care package took shape. Practitioners were advised to look thoughtfully at a person's way of living and consider personal factors such as level of motivation, since such indicators would inform how care plans were to take shape (p62). Alternatives and options were to be fully discussed. The first three action points on the checklist for practitioners implementing a care plan reflect these precepts:

1. Has the user been involved to the limit of their capacity in the implementation process?

2. Have the inputs of users and carers been maximised and have formal service inputs been geared to their support? In other words, have the ways in which users and carers draw on their own particular strengths and personal resources been recognised and encouraged, and have these been linked to services which support and do not take over?

3. Has the pace of implementation been agreed with the user?
   (SSI, DoH, 1991a, page 76)

Revised guidelines on care planning within the SAP similarly promote user-centred and user-friendly concepts as described above. Further, concepts which embrace equal opportunities principles and practices in the delivery of social care are also an integral part of this new framework. Good practice requires that Adult Social Services need to develop policies, implement codes of practice and procedures, train staff and monitor practice, in order to identify ways in which minority or disadvantaged groups are not directly or indirectly discriminated against (Orme, 2000). The following quotation from government guidance (Department of Health 2002b, annex E, Stages of assessment) describes those indicators of which practitioners need to be alert when constructing care plans:

> *Care planning should be responsive to – but not prejudiced against – the age, living circumstances, geographic location, disabilities, gender, culture, faith, personal relationships and lifestyle choices of service users. Care planning should build on the strengths and abilities of individuals and the part they can play in addressing their needs. It should address external or environmental factors that have caused the need to arise, or will hamper the resolutions of need if not addressed.*
> (Department of Health, 2002b, page 24)

A care plan grounded in reality

Then as now, the care plan was to be grounded in reality. In 1991 the aim of the care planning stage was 'to target intervention as precisely as possible on the identified needs' (SSI, Department of Health, 1991a, page 62). Service requirements were to reflect the level of risk assessed and agreed between all parties (see the section on risk assessment below). Objectives were to be clearly spelt out together with the criteria for measuring a positive outcome. Payne (1995) describes the need to have a *sense of strategy* in order to understand *where the care plan is coming from and its future overall direction* (page 112).

Differences between the user, carer, practitioner or other agency were to be recorded; details of the named person responsible for implementing, monitoring and reviewing the care plan was to be provided; those involved were to be clear about the factors which may trigger an early review and the user was to have a copy of the document (SSI, Department of Health, 1991a, page 67). This good practice remains in the SAP (see below). Further, the cost of the care plan was and is fully recorded, reflecting the costs to the user and the agencies. Putting together the cost of the care plan has important local and national policy implications within a culture of resource contraints and accountability. You may find the following background information helpful in explaining the context to the current position on resourcing the care plan. This is not neutral territory and resources discussed in Chapter 1 and below affect how the objectives of a care plan are shaped.

Nationally driven resource constraints and links with care planning for adults

Care management is seen as the vehicle for targeting services within a framework of welfare which is driven by resource constraints and accountability (Hughes, 1995; McDonald, 2006). Commentators such as Waterson (1999) reflect that community care assessments have become focused on risk management and limiting services to those cases which carry a high risk and that this approach of *containing risks becomes a means of rationing scarce resources* (page 276). Indeed, when setting the eligibility criteria the local authority is able to put constraints on need by taking into account what can be afforded before a need is assessed. This is a disputed area. For details of landmark legal cases which may be in conflict with the Human Rights Act (see Brayne and Carr, 2005 page 547).

If you the service user thought you needed and would be better off in a desirable (more expensive) residential home for adults with a sea view, your Adult Social Services may define your needs in the light of local resource constraints, and decide that a different (less expensive) home is appropriate and write the care plan accordingly. You would of course be able to live in the home of your choice, providing you could pay the difference between the two fees.

Nonetheless, under Fair Access to Care Services (Department of Health, 2002c) as from April 2003, the government increased Adult Social Services spending power in real terms by six per cent per annum. This is designed to enable more people in genuine need to receive support.

Users' contribution towards care costs

Financial assessment of a service user's means may be an integral part of the care plan depending on local policies on charging for care (see item 10 of the SAP below). Some practitioners view charging for care services as difficult since it may not rest well with some social work principles. Trained to help service users to maximise their income through, for example, the take up of benefits, they find themselves, often uncomfortably so, in the role of gate keepers to scarce resources (Bradley and Manthorpe, 1997). Research indicated (Bradley, 2003) that practitioners sometimes experience dilemmas and conflicts of interest between older people, their relatives and the local authority when undertaking financial assessments for long term care. Variations in charging for home-based care were identified in two official reports: *Report of the Royal Commission on long term care* (1999) and the Audit Commission's *Charging with care* (2000). According to the government it was these reports that prompted it to act and produce a local authority circular (LAC (2001) 32) entitled *Fairer charging policies for home care and other non-residential social services* (Department of Health, 2001b). The following provides you with some factual information on the charging system within care planning.

Charging service users for services within the care plan – and fair access to care services

A fully costed care plan within care management, then and now, may reflect the contribution made by the service user. At the point when the care plan is being shaped the care manager will be responsible for making a decision concerning the contribution from the service user. Whilst NHS services remain free of charge, Adult Social Services have discretion and may charge for community home based care services. Charges for the non-nursing component (that is personal care and residency costs) of care in long stay homes in England and Wales are levied, on a means tested basis using nationally agreed thresholds. There are two areas where Adult Social Services are not allowed to charge and these concern the assessment of need and general advice on community care, and also after care services of mental health patients under the Mental Health Act 1983 s.117. Further, people who are terminally ill with a prognosis of less than six weeks to live normally receive a free service and those eligible for intermediate care (a service that provides for intensive support and rehabilitation following hospital discharge) normally recieve a free service for the first six weeks.

Under the guidelines (Department of Health, 2002c; Department of Health, 2002d) which promote fairer charging policies for home care, charges levied by local councils must be reasonable, consistent with good practice in social care and not result in the service user being worse off financially than they were before the changes. The aim of Fair Access to Care Services (Department of Health, 2002c) is to create a more consistent and equitable approach to implementing eligibility criteria by introducing a national framework within which local authorities should establish local eligibility criteria. Thus it stops short of establishing national criteria on eligibility which is seen as a limitation (see Lymbery 2005 page 158 for a fuller discussion). Nonetheless, some significant progress has been made. The changes were introduced in two phases. Firstly, local authorities were required to act by October 2002, and remove charges from service users in receipt of a range of income and disability linked benefits. As part of the financial assessment of income service users with a significant disability receive *an individual assessment of their disability–related expenditure* (LAC (2001) 32, s.2.3) since it is assumed that having a disability is likely to give rise to more expensive living costs, such as heating charges. Secondly more sensitive approaches to charging for home care were implemented by April 2003. Good practice dictates that following the decisions reached concerning the care plan, service users will be assessed on their ability to pay and given information on the charges before the service is provided. Details of the charging policy should be published and made available to the public (Department of Health, 2002c). Detailed practice guidance on fair access to care services was published by the Department of Health in 2003 (see 2003b).

In spite of the considerable developments in fairer charging this area of work can be challenging for practitioners. Adults who currently have savings over £21,000 are viewed as 'self funders' and whilst they may opt to purchase services privately, without a formal assessment, care plan or system of monitoring services, they may be vulnerable. On the other hand they are likely to have more choice than people on a low income. The latter can be at the mercy of some local authority policies that, for example, may hold the line on only delivering frozen meals, never providing cleaning, and only offering assisted baths on a weekly basis.

The care plan and 2002 guidance
In 2002, guidance for the care plan within the SAP framework appears set to make certain that health and social care personnel and overlapping procedures for vulnerable older people work effectively. Clarity concerning which agency is responsible for which service is a key driver. The recommendation is that if a nursing plan is required, it is to be fully integrated into the overall plan, reflecting the need for the 'joined up' service. A key requirement is for everything to be written down, including the extent to which the service user accepts a degree of risk, no doubt reflecting our increasingly 'risk averse' society.

Care plans according to the SAP process should include:

1. A summary of identified/eligible needs indicating the intensity, instability, predictability, and complexity of needs, the associated risks to independence and the potential for rehabilitation.

2. A note whether or not the service user has agreed the care plan and a reason where this was not possible.

3. A note on whether or not the user has consented for care plan information to be shared among relevant agencies and a reason where this was not possible.

4. The objectives of providing help and anticipated outcomes for users.

5. A summary of how services will impact on identified/eligible need and associated risks.

6. The part the user will play in addressing needs, including the strengths and abilities they will bring to this.

7. Details of managing risk as appropriate. Where it has been argued that users will accept a certain degree of risk, this must be written into the care plan.

8. Details of what carers are willing to do, and related needs and support.

9. A description of the level and frequency of the help that is to be provided, stating which agency is responsible for what service.

10. Details of any contributions to care costs that users are asked to make.

11. A nursing plan (integrated not attached) where appropriate.

12. The level of Registered Nurse Care Contribution for admissions to care homes which provide nursing care.

13. The name of the person co-ordinating the care plan and their contact number.

14. A contact number or office in case of emergencies and a contingency plan if things go wrong.

15. Monitoring arrangements and a date for review.
    (Department of Health, 2002b, annex E, page 24)

Constructing the care plan for adults

We have drawn your attention to the guidance and some of the principles on which care planning is based in adult services. In this section we elaborate further on some key practice related issues and concepts prior to setting some learning exercises for you in care planning. For example we shall consider the perspective of the carer, the importance of risk assessment and ways in which models of disability can inform the construction of the care plan.

In each Adult Social Services, similar and detailed administrative procedures are in place to guide practitioners and enable them to complete a range of care planning forms. The process is intended to be systematic and transparent. It is anticipated that each professional involved in the SAP will be clear about what they are expected to do and that this will not be left to, for example, a casual and unrecorded talk on the telephone. All aspects of the care plan will be costed and communicated in written format to those with formal responsibilities. The new emphasis is on specifying the practical results of the process, these are known as the outcomes. Being certain about the criteria for measuring outcomes is also part of the care planning process. The reasons and factors that may trigger an early review of the care plan are to be known to all who are involved in its construction.

A person centred approach

As with the assessment process, care planning is an art as well as a science. Care managers will use their judgement, practice skills and experience to decide how the process should be completed. It is not always a straightforward procedure. Ideas for the care plan will be shaped whilst the levels of dependency banding from the assessment process are being worked through. Much will depend on the quality of the relationship forged between the key workers and the service users. Care managers will need to develop a trusting and sincere relationship with the service user if they are to gather an understanding of a *typical day in the life of*. In so doing they draw on skills that are referred to as helping skills (Bradley, 1997, Egan, 2001) that of recent are more commonly described as 'person centred'. These skills are based on values such as trust, compassion, empathy and openness that have long been at the heart of social work practice (Payne, 2005). A person centred approach has become part of the government's vision (Department of Health, 2005) for the delivery of social care for adults in England. Care managers will need to find out what is feasible and desirable; intricate details of what the service user wants and is capable of doing for themselves. This may involve challenging the service user to be more realistic about their current reality; perhaps recognising, for example, that willingness to agree to a care plan may be linked with the desire of the service user to be discharged more speedily from hospital.

The point of view of the carer

When the success of the care package relies on the goodwill and input of an informal carer, talking to them about their wishes and preferences and undertaking a separate assessment of their needs under the 1995 Carers (Recognition and Services) Act (CRSA) is likely to be of vital importance. Under the provision of the Carers and Disabled Children Act (2000) (CDCA), local authorities can take preventative and supportive action to help carers by, for example, making payments to them directly for their services, and stepping in to allow them to take a break. The right of a carer to have their own independent life fully recognised has become a statutory requirement in the Carers (Equal Opportunities) Act 2004 and accessing services that enable he/she to have a more balanced life needs to be an integral part of assessment and care planning (Brayne and Carr, 2005 p.530). Further good practice guidance that empahsises the full involvement of the carer alongside that of the service user in assessment and care planning has been placed within a legal framework following a recent local authority circular (see LAC (2004) 24: *The Community Care Assessment Directions* 2004).

Risk assessment and elder abuse

The stages of the SAP listed above indicate that risk assessment and risk management are integral aspects of the process. When putting together the care plan McDonald (2006, page 51) reminds us that assessing risk is *a balancing process in which the application of judgement is brought to bear*. The process is one in which the likelihood of an event happening and its foreseeable consequences and the interests of those people affected by the consequences, are balanced against the costs of taking precautions and sometimes over-robust interventions may override the expressed wishes of the service user. So for example, a service user in a similar position to Gladys Beaumont may be persuaded not to return home from hospital but be admitted into a 'less risky' environment such as a residential home. Risk assessment must not however be dismissed and should be an integral part of all assessments of vulnerable adults. It is an important tool for practitioners to monitor and be alert to a range of consequences, for example, elder abuse. This concept has not been well reported and may take several forms; emotional, physical and financial. It is not limited to one age group, gender or culture and yet older people living alone may be more likely to suffer from financial abuse and neglect at the hands of others (McCreadie, 1996). However more recently local authorities, drawing on Department of Health guidance (2000b) have developed 'No Secrets' policies and procedures that may have an impact on assessment and care plans. If, for example, abuse is suspected then this could trigger an adult abuse investigation that is likely to require specific social work skills. For a fuller explanation and exploration of abuse of vulnerable adults see Crawford and Walker's (2004) chapter on 'Vulnerability and abuse'.

Mental Capacity Act 2005

If Gladys Beaumont was confused and beginning to lose her ability to make decisions for herself, perhaps as a result of developing dementia, then you as her care manager would need to be informed about the new Mental Capacity Act 2005 when carrying out an assessment and constructing a care plan. This Act provides a statutory framework to protect and empower vulnerable people who are not able to make decisions for themselves. It clarifies who is able to make these decisions, in which circumstances and how the nominated person can go about this. The Act also enables the potentially vulnerable person to plan ahead for a time when they may not have the capacity to act in an informed way. Guidance in the form of a Code of Practice is linked to the Act and refers to those working in a professional capacity, such as doctors and social workers, who have a duty to have regard to the code. Further guidance and detail on the Act can be found on the Department of Health's website: www.dh.gov.uk/.

Underpinning concepts that inform the care plan

When putting together care plans the practitioner needs to be aware of underpinning concepts that inform good practice. For example, the concept of normalisation which we referred to in Chapter 1 aims to enable people to live a life with similar day-to-day rhythms to others in their community. This approach was developed with the needs of people with learning difficulties in mind (Wolfensberger, 1972). It is equally valid when considering care plans for older people who may not wish, for example, to rise or go to bed purely at the convenience of the service providers. Being required to go to bed early and not being able to do ordinary things in habitual ways such as watching a favourite late night TV programme from the comfort of a particular chair in a known room, may be a high price to pay and may send the signal that life is no longer 'normal'. Similarly, when drawing up a care plan for a person with severe disabilities, such as Gladys Beaumont, care managers should be aware of the models of disability which inform our perceptions. The challenge is not to fall into 'disablist perceptions' by accepting the medical model of disability which focuses on physical deficits and on individual health needs. Oliver (1996) encourages us to look more objectively at the extent to which our society has helped to compound disability through insensitive and inaccessible infrastructures, such as public transport systems, for example buses that are not constructed to be used by people in wheelchairs. Drawing on ideas from the social model of disability may help practitioners to challenge why, for example, particular forms of public transport are inaccessible for service users such as Gladys Beaumont. As care managers employed by a local authority, practitioners are in a strong position to raise concerns through their line managers which may be taken up at director level between appropriate agencies.

A critique of the practice of care planning

There are challenges in putting good practice precepts and the interests of the service user uppermost into care planning practice. User empowerment, referred to in an earlier section, implies power sharing and self-management by users and involves a philosophy which spurns unnecessary bureaucracy (Adams, 2003). Care planning within a system of care management operates within a 'top down' system of local authority power and control in which according to Lymbery (1998) *the professional components of care management are clearly subordinate to the administrative and managerial requirements* (p873). In other words, the role of the care manager has become more and more rule bound and bureaucratic. Research (Postle, 2001; Bradley, 2005) points to care managers becoming overwhelmed by bureaucracy and paperwork with decreasing amount of face-to-face time spent with service users with less opportunity to use their interpersonal skills. Whilst the SAP may go some way to rationalise the spread of paper, it is unlikely that this elaborate form of assessment and planning will not require a high level of top-down administration.

For further elaboration and detail on the practitioner's role in care planning, we suggest you read relevant chapters in Payne's (1995) *Social work and community care* and McDonald's (2006) *Understanding community care: a guide for social workers*.

ACTIVITY **3.3**

Care planning for Gladys Beaumont: constructing key aspects of the care plan

1. *In order to keep the task relatively simple we focus on item nine of the care plan in the SAP which is a description of the level and frequency of the help that is to be provided, stating which agency is responsible for what service. In order to break down this task, we ask you first to think creatively about Gladys Beaumont's probable daily needs on her return home and complete a daily/weekly chart (see below) from a professional/agency perspective, indicating which professional is likely to walk down the garden path to do what, when and how, and when and where Gladys is likely to go to receive treatment. We suggest that you take copies of this chart since it may be useful to make several drafts and you need further copies for item two below. We have already mentioned some*

of the professionals who are likely to be involved (see Chapter 1); there will be a care assistant from a home care agency to help with personal and daily living tasks and you may think of others. It is unlikely however that those professionals who are hospital based will continue to care for Gladys, and she is likely to receive, for example, physio-therapy and perhaps occupational therapy from other workers attached to her local health centre or in the outpatient department at the local hospital.

In order to accomplish this task you will need to be practical and consider the detailed ways in which Gladys is likely to live her life in her changed circumstances on returning home. What are her views and preferences; her strengths, weaknesses and level of moti-vation; her personal and physical needs? Think of things that could go wrong in the plan and possible contingencies you could draw on to build in more support. Draft a day-to-day plan of agency/worker involvement that you think and feel will be acceptable to Gladys, one that is multidisciplinary, given her health needs, and realistic in terms of man-aging risk without stifling her independence. Have you thought about the security of the bungalow and how the professionals would get inside her home? Challenge yourself – will your care plan enable Gladys to be safe, comfortable and as independent as possible at home? In spite of the uncertainties, having a plan is still the best option because it gives you a base line from which to monitor and adjust the support needed.

In order to guide you we provide some key objectives for the plan which should give you a steer concerning how a care plan is likely to take shape. The objectives are:

- *To continue to encourage Gladys in her rehabilitation and work towards her becoming more physically independent and mobile.*

- *To actively seek to help Gladys to change her diet and fully stabilise her diabetes.*

- *To encourage Gladys to lead a more creative and positive life in her community.*

- *To assess the extent to which the six-week trial of the pendant alarm* has been successful.*

- *To review the care plan in six weeks or sooner if the home care arrangements break down for any reason.*

  * An electronic device that a vulnerable person may attach to their garments, or wear round the neck or on a wrist so that in an emergency help can be summoned. The pendant is normally linked to a 24-hour call service.

You may wish to add more objectives.

2. *Using the same chart, think yourself into Gladys' social network. Drawing on the origi-nal assessment in Chapter 1 and pulling out some of the ideas from Chapter 4 concerning Gladys' crisis management, complete a daily/weekly chart which reflects the support and resources from her informal network. Be certain to build in activities which are 'doable', given her disabilities, and which will enhance Gladys' quality of life. Now link the two charts together. Are they complementary? Is the daily plan too professionally dominated? Does it stifle Gladys and prevent her getting on with aspects of her life which she has now decided are important to her? If this is the case, can you adjust plan A?*

Care plan: schedule of daily and weekly tasks

| | Date compiled: | | Service user: | | Overall criteria: | | |
	Monday	Tuesday	Wednesday	Thursday	Friday	Saturday	Sunday
Early morning							
Mid-morning							
Lunch							
Mid-afternoon							
Late afternoon							
Evening							
Bedtime							
Night							

3. We ask you to set down supplementary objectives for each of the five key objectives listed above. The supplementary objectives should be measurable, able to be reassessed when the case is reviewed and also provide you with a 'road map' to guide your care plan. For example in objective one, you may wish to think about how often Gladys might be able to see a physiotherapist, the type of exercises she should be practising at home, whether it is feasible to aim for her being able to transfer her weight by the next review. This would be a criterion for measuring a positive outcome *as mentioned earlier, but it may be too optimistic. There are many uncertainties about this case (as there are with real life cases) and much depends on factors which are hard to assess accurately at the outset. For example, the exact nature of Gladys' medical condition. We recognise that in developing the complex case of Gladys Beaumont we require you to have some under-standing of health related matters, a common occurrence in care management practice. If you are uncertain about Gladys' medical position, you could ask a health professional in your local community. Alternatively for further information you may wish to access the NHS website, see: **cks.library.nhs.uk**

4. You may also like to consider how you would explain the plan to Gladys and reach a writ-ten agreement with her and the people involved in her care.

5. Finally, returning to item nine in the SAP, in the light of daily and weekly living charts which you have worked at, provide a description of the level and frequency of the help that is to be provided, stating which agency is responsible for what service. We have pro-vided a second chart in order to help you construct your response.

ACTIVITY **3.3** *continued*

Care plan – level and frequency of help

Date compiled:	Service user:	Overall banding:
Level of task	Frequency of help	Agency/worker responsible

Care plan sequences and outcomes

Apart from the care provided, there are several outcomes to a care plan which Payne (1995) draws our attention to. He reflects that:

Less obvious outcomes may include the feelings and responses of the people involved in providing and receiving the care; actual effects of the service on the clients and the people around them; information which may affect the planning and management of services more widely; changes in the way agencies work; changes in the community which surround the client and how it responds to problems in its midst...
(Payne, 1995, page 112)

These thoughts provide insights into what the skilled care manager will be checking out and monitoring as they build up a picture of what is working in the care plan and what remains at the level of a wish and a desire. We shall return to these ideas in Chapter 5 when we consider the reviewing process. Finally, we describe the case study in terms of the decisions that we would make concerning Gladys Beaumont. How do they compare with your analysis?

Gladys Beaumont – a realistic care plan?

Matthew finally agrees, with Gladys' consent, to a package of home care, which will include care staff visiting up to three times each day. He describes this as the 'enabling service' that will run for the next six weeks during which time care workers will 'assist and encourage, rather than 'do for' Gladys. Gladys has agreed that her attendance allowance (AA), which she has recently applied for, will contribute towards the cost of the package. She knows that she will still be means tested and has agreed to see a benefits worker to gain independent advice.

In working out the charge for home care, Matthew has also taken into account the extra expenses which Gladys is likely to have, for heating and special dietary needs, as a consequence of her disability (see LAC (2001) 32, section 2.3 discussed above). A personal carer will visit in the morning between 8 and 8.30 a.m. to help get Gladys up, dressed and prepare breakfast; once at lunch time when 'meals on wheels' are not being delivered (the plan is for five meals on wheels a week) and once at 6 p.m. to help her prepare a light snack. Janice (her neighbour) will receive some training from the O.T. in order to help Gladys into bed at a mutually convenient time. Gladys has agreed to a six-week trial of a pendant alarm linked to 24-hour cover. Samantha the District Nurse says that she will visit weekly to keep an eye on her health and diet, since the aim is to encourage Gladys to be independent in terms of managing her diabetes and medication. Gladys is to continue with weekly physiotherapy at the local health centre. Janice will also continue to help Gladys with her shopping and encourage her to buy healthier food. Gladys has agreed to Janice's suggestion that she take her to the local park in her wheelchair to watch the bowling, and also visit the local garden centre. Gladys' niece, Anthea, has agreed to do the washing on a weekly basis. She too has been taught by the O.T. how to help transfer her aunt into her car, so that they can go out together. The people from the local church who visited Gladys on the ward have said that they will stay in contact and include her in church events. Janice and the niece have a key to the bungalow and the local authority has fitted a 'key safe' (a box for the key, with a code, fitted outside the front door) and charged Gladys £25. This enables the care workers to access the house. The pressure is on to discharge Gladys as soon as possible since she is now very motivated to return home.

A major uncertainty remains – will Gladys' mobility improve, will she be able to transfer herself, walk on crutches or even learn to walk again with a prosthesis? In the light of this uncertainty how realistic is it to install rails outside the bungalow? Matthew recognises that in drawing up the care plan he has been guided by his health colleagues and that their judgement and knowledge of Gladys' condition has been essential. Nonetheless all involved recognise that there is a level of risk which appears to be manageable although Matthew feels that too much of the plan rests on the good will of Janice. Gladys is in full agreement with the plan, and gives her signature to a form which also outlines Matthew's concerns about the ongoing risks. Full written details are also shared with all parties and details of the plan and emergency contact numbers are left on the hall table in the bungalow, in accordance with SAP guidance.

C H A P T E R   S U M M A R Y

In this chapter we have considered how information gained and negotiated during an assessment contributes to the development of a plan to meet needs. Again, it is important that social workers practise in ways that include service users at the centre of the work. Plans in respect of child and family social work and work with adults have been introduced, set within the context in which you will be developing them and illustrated by reference to case study material. Following the development of a plan social workers and service users work towards its implementation. In the next chapter we will consider some of the ways in which plans can be operationalised.

It may help, in any plan that you are involved in constructing, to remember the acronym HOSEC:

- be **h**onest about the reasons for the plan;

- be **o**pen about who does what and what 'comebacks' there might be;

- be **s**imple in your use of language;

- be **e**xplicit about what it is that you are communicating;

- be **c**lear in your written expression.

FURTHER READING

Department of Health, Department for Education and Employment, Home Office (2000) Framework for the assessment of children in need and their families. London: The Stationery Office.

Laming, H (2003) The Victoria Climbié inquiry report. Cm 5730. London: The Stationery Office.

The report into the tragic death of Victoria Climbié is essential reading for all social work students and qualified practitioners regardless of area of practice. The lessons learned for assessment, planning and communicating must be learned and applied.

McDonald, A (2006) Understanding Community Care: a guide for social workers. Basingstoke, Palgrave, Macmillan.

This is an accessible, practice oriented guide and overview of community care.

Payne, M (1995) Social work and Community Care. Basingstoke: Macmillan.

This book provides a thorough grounding in the underlying principles and good practice initiatives in community care.

Chapter 4
Intervening to make a difference

Introduction

In this chapter you will explore some ways in which social workers put in place plans made with service users to achieve agreed goals. The chapter will introduce you to a range of interventions including task-centred practice, cognitive behavioural approaches, crisis intervention, networking and advocacy. You will be asked to consider and reflect on these interventions. It is important to remember that interventions are simply tools for a particular purpose and that the intervention, model or approach should not lead but the service user's needs remain paramount.

You will be invited to consider how to construct and implement an intervention plan in child and family work and work with adults. Issues arising from 'voluntary' and 'involuntary' use of services will be explored. Guidance, research and advice on intervening effectively will be provided and activities will help you to make links between knowledge and practice throughout this chapter. A particular focus will concern the recording of interventions and associated processes. The importance of simple recording schedules and making your written recording style easy to read will be considered. Service user involvement in the intervention process will be emphasised through student centred activities.

Theory, methods and models: contested debates

Debates about theory, models and methods in social work practice are complex and contested. It can be a difficult and taxing area for students to make sense of. It has, unfortunately, led to many students abandoning an explicit use of models and methods in practice and a false and unhelpful divide being created between theories, models, methods and practice. Some of the initial comments made by the Minister for Health, when the social work degree was introduced, appeared to echo an anti-theoretical approach. However, in the foreword to the Department of Health (2002a) *Requirements for social work training* the emphasis is on competence in practice which necessarily employs knowledge, theories and methods.

> *The new award will require social workers to demonstrate their practical application of skills and knowledge and their ability to deliver a service that creates opportunities for service users. It will require all social workers to demonstrate their knowledge of human growth and development, particularly development of children and other vulnerable groups, their communication skills and their ability to work confidently and effectively with other professionals. The emphasis must be on practice and the practical relevance of theory.*
> (Department of Health, 2002a, page i)

Trevithick (2005) considers three interconnected domains of knowledge that are important in social work practice:

- Theoretical knowledge

- Factual knowledge

- Practice knowledge.

It will be useful briefly to explore each of these in turn, (see box 4)

Box 4: Types of Knowledge in Social Work
Theoretical knowledge
In social work the theoretical base is predominated by knowledge borrowed from other disciplines. It has been suggested that this might make the interpretation and use of such knowledge difficult because it is taken out of context. It may also be the case that the knowledge is limited as it generally developed within Western frameworks and assumptions and may not apply well to diverse cultures and societies. The core elements of borrowed knowledge come from psychology, sociology, law, philosophy, medicine, political and economic science.

Theoretical knowledge may also refer to theories that analyse the tasks and purposes of social work, or to approaches to practice, sometimes called practice theories or models. Theoretical knowledge relies on theory. Theories themselves remain hypothetical rather than absolute, attempting to explain, predict and illuminate from a range of perspectives.

Factual knowledge refers to data, statistics, figures, records and research findings. It is important not to be immediately accepting of the veracity of these 'facts' or the implications that might seem to arise from them. Trevithick (2005) points to the important rule of 'falsification' attributed to Karl Popper. Data must be able to be scrutinised, checked and be open to falsification if it is to be accepted as scientific. There are elements of factual knowledge that, for social workers, are crucial. One might immediately think of knowledge of legislation relating to your particular field of practice, knowledge of resources available in your area, knowledge of the procedures of the agency that guide practice.

Finally, practice knowledge relates to the use of self and the importance of a critical perspective in your use of knowledge, skills of reasoning and practice. Pawson et al. (2003) recognised that practitioner knowledge is usually passed on in a tacit way and acquired through practice and sharing collective wisdom, through training and formal and informal consultation rather than judged against any specific standards. Practice wisdom and working intuitively lie at the heart of reflective practice, which underpins much of what social workers do and how their practice develops. However, it does not make explicit why social workers do what they do and what works in practice.

One of the difficulties in considering social work methods was highlighted by Marsh and Triseliotis (1996) who found that students and practitioners could identify many different models and methods for social work practice, but there was no agreement on which should be used in which circumstances. The 'art' and 'science' debate that we referred to in Chapter 1 permeates the argument about and use of theories and methods. Arguments have become polarised to some extent between those who point out that social work is an ever-changing profession and those who have adopted an evidence-based approach to practice. The former group would suggest that because social work responds to uncertainties, complexities and contradictions in human life it cannot be bound to a particular model for practice. The latter group might, on the other hand, suggest the only models for practice are those which can be shown to do what they say they will do.

RESEARCH SUMMARY

Trotter's empirical model of social work practice

Trotter (1999) proposes a model that is based on empirical evidence of success. It involves practitioners in carrying out their own single-case experiments on their casework.

He argues that critics of empirical practice state that:

- *it is reductionist – it breaks human life into small chunks without seeing the wider perspective;*

- *value-based and individual objectives might be ignored because they are not open to the measurement demanded by evidence-based practice;*

RESEARCH SUMMARY

- *they provide* one best answer, *and therefore downplay diversity.*

Social work, however, is a complex activity and often workers and service users have multiple objectives to pursue. Empirical models of practice, in fact, rest on the values of starting where the service user is at; of acknowledging the importance of presenting problems and working together openly and honestly to find solutions.

Approaches that work are characterised by clear, honest and frequent discussions about the role of the worker and the client. There is an important focus on modelling and encouraging the expression of pro-social behaviours and actions by the client. The use of a collaborative problem-solving approach that focuses on the client's definitions of problems and goals is also indicated.

Effective models of practice, according to Trotter, include the following.

a) Ecological systems theory: *this emphasises the interrelatedness of people and events and the impact that intervening in one system might have on another system. The theory also recognises the importance of roles that individuals adopt.*

b) Behavioural and cognitive-behavioural theory: *these theories acknowledge the influence of the actions of others, modelling and the importance of thoughts and feelings in the production of behaviours and responses.*

c) Feminist casework: *this focuses on the way in which patriarchy disadvantages women through sex role stereotyping and the devaluing of women's experiences.*

d) Radical casework: *acknowledges the importance of structural factors influencing the client's situation.*

e) Task-centred casework: *this uses a problem-solving focus.*

f) Solution-focused approaches: *these focus on client strengths and solutions rather than problem areas.*

Evidence-based approaches have been adapted from scientific disciplines and medicine. They propose that only those models which can be shown to work and do what they claim they can do should be learned and applied by social work students. Whilst the latter approach may appear self-evident, it is clear that social workers do operate in complex and ever-changing situations. The two approaches rely on different ways of understanding social work and social life. These different understandings are important because they influence policy developments which, in turn, affect what is done in practice and, therefore, what outcomes occur. However, the two approaches may not be as sharply polarised as seems at first glance. It is unlikely that a practitioner who favours an approach that takes change and uncertainty into account would not wish their intervention to work! It is equally unlikely to think that a practitioner using evidence-based approaches would believe that situations do not change and that a range of factors – such as motivation, physical and mental health, prior experiences, family situation and cultural heritage – would not influence the methods used.

A further important factor complicating the use of social work methods comes from our understanding of social work. The question 'what is social work?' is often asked and qualified practitioners, student social workers and academics have consistently failed to decide what it is. These questions are debated in Horner (2006). Whilst teachers *teach*, nurses *nurse*, managers *manage* and police officers *police*, agreement on what social workers do is lacking. We are not certain that social work can be understood as a discrete profession globally in a similar way, perhaps, to medicine. Social work necessarily relies on local interpretations often at the level of agency practice. There are some common elements of social work in the UK, however. It is clear that social workers work with vulnerable people in society who are in some way marginalised or excluded from full participation in society. They also work with the context in which people live, including other people around an individual, the physical environment and with other services working with that person. Social workers work to improve the life chances of people in their living environment. This is something not undertaken by other professions. In order to work effectively, social workers need to equip themselves with a range of methods for practice that work to reduce social exclusion, increase life chances and opportunities, and to demonstrate that effectiveness in practice.

A further issue is raised by the wide range of possible models and methods available and a lack of clarity or obscuring of the theories underlying these models. See for instance the 14 models identified by Watson and West (2006, pages 53–54). Whichever model is used, however, it is clear that service users appreciate an approach that is empathic, appears genuine and displays warmth. Service users also want social workers to be honest and up-front. They do not want to be faced with hidden agendas and unexpected consequences.

The intention in this chapter is to introduce a range of models that may assist social workers in achieving desired and agreed outcomes for service users. These models will be framed by the understanding that social workers operate at many different levels in society – with individuals, families, groups and communities – and, therefore an overall approach is needed that understands the ways in which the various elements of social life interact and interconnect. We will briefly introduce a *systems* approach to social life. It is also acknowledged that certain basic helping skills are central to effective deployment of methods and models for practice whether these derive from a fluid, person-centred approach or an evidence-based perspective.

A systems approach

In Chapter 2 you examined the first principles of the systems approach in relation to ecomaps (see page 47). Whilst systems thinking came originally from biology and has been developed in increasingly complex ways, it is important to note that in social work systems thinking has emphasised the interactive context of social life. Individuals are not seen as isolated, unconnected beings but social and affected by and influencing others around them, the organisations with which they have contact and, indeed, wider society (Payne, 2005).

This acknowledgement is important because it recognises that a child in need or an older person with failing health affects those around them and that the response of those around them affects their well-being or otherwise. It goes wider than this, however, and links to social workers' commitment to anti-oppressive practice that understands oppression to be multi-directional and not simply personal prejudice directed by one person towards another (Dominelli, 2002; Thompson, 2002). A systems approach considers the impact that social structures, the kinds of help and support provided and access to them have on the ways in which individuals, families, groups and communities respond. It is important to reiterate that social workers operate at the edges of society, assisting those who are in some way disenfranchised from participating in society. This means, therefore, that social workers need to keep the many levels and directions of interaction in mind when intervening as a social worker. Systems thinking does not offer an explanation of the reasons why things happen and does not really provide a model of intervention.

Core helping skills

Research conducted concerning service user satisfaction and the ways in which people wish to be treated by social work professionals consistently highlights some of the core interpersonal communication and helping skills (Koprowska, 2006).

Those core helping skills were first articulated by Carl Rogers (1951; 1961), a humanist psychologist, and, despite, being refined and added to remain central today. The basic qualities of helping relationships are well known and comprise:

- empathy;
- warmth;
- genuineness.

Carkhuff (1987) adds three more essential conditions to the helping relationship:

- concreteness;
- immediacy;
- confrontation.

A brief overview of these qualities is shown below.

Core qualities for helping relationships

Empathy represents the ability to experience the world of another person as if it was one's own without actually losing the 'as if' quality. An important way of beginning to demonstrate empathy is to reflect the content of what is said and adjust your understanding accordingly. However, it is not content alone that you are seeking to understand but the whole experience of the person. Therefore, social workers also need to reflect feelings; the aim being to check the congruence of feelings expressed with the content of what is said: whether feelings and contents match each other.

Warmth, also known as unconditional positive regard or acceptance, is shown by respecting people for what they are as unique individuals and creating a safe and trusting environment in which service users can express themselves. Showing acceptance for people in all situations can be difficult but is central to effective helping.

Genuineness relates to directness and openness in the social worker's communication. The social worker does not have hidden agendas, concealed thoughts or pretend but encourages direct and open communication.

Concreteness refers to specificity. The practitioner ensures that the person they are helping is specific about the particular meanings they attach to their ideas, images, thoughts, feelings and descriptions. It adds clarity to the communication and facilitates the practitioner checking their understanding of the person in need.

Immediacy suggests that it is important not to spend too much time in talk about the past and past behaviours but to focus on the immediate and central problem or issue of concern.

Confrontation concerns the pointing out of discrepancies and disconfirmatory evidence between the social worker's view and the service user's. Common discrepancies include differences between the real and ideal view of the self, differences between the person's thinking and feelings and what they actually do in practice and differences between the real world as seen by the practitioner and the fantasy world as seen by the person in need.

These qualities are important, but are conveyed using learnt interpersonal or helping skills. When engaging in a social work relationship with a service user, social workers should be mindful of the needs of service users. Egan (2001) identifies some of the important interpersonal skills necessary for effective helping:

- attending;
- listening;
- probing;
- effective challenging.

These skills build on the qualities listed above.

A social worker being present at an important point in another person's life can make a big difference. Effective attending lets service users know that you were there and were prepared to listen. Being attentive, however, involves becoming aware of how you sit, how the room is positioned, how much eye contact you make and your own level of comfort in the situation. It also demands that you attend to the ways in which you use your body language and the messages being communicated to you by the service user's body language. What is important is that you do not become so wrapped up in interpreting body language that you miss the overt messages. The key is to be natural and relaxed as far as possible but to practise recognition of your use of body language in a safe environment. You will soon be able to apply the skills learnt in a natural way. It is important to remember that you speak with colleagues every day. The skills used are similar to those applied in social work situations.

Listening is a far more complex skill than simply hearing what it is that the other person is saying. It involves being attentive to the feelings expressed when speaking, the gaps, silences, hesitations and pauses. According to Egan (2001), listening involves the following.

- Observing and reading the service user's non-verbal behaviour – this involves being mindful of our own non-verbal behaviour and recognising that there are different cultural norms and that assumptions should not be made. Check out your understanding.

- Listening to and understanding the service user's verbal messages. This again demands summarising, checking and amending your understanding as appropriate.

- Listening to the whole person in the context of social settings of their life. People develop understanding on the basis of their experiences, environment, culture and personalities. As a social worker, it is important to acknowledge the range of influences on people.

- Tough-minded listening. Social workers can only help people effectively if they are prepared to confront discrepancies and demonstrate their honest and clear approach.

These interpersonal skills are important whatever methods of intervention are used, and the deployment and use of them should begin at the outset of your relationship with service users.

ACTIVITY *4.1*

It is important to become more aware of how you present to other people and what messages you might convey. Choose a colleague or friend and ask if they would help you to begin examining your communication skills.

Spend about 20 minutes talking together about a topic of general interest to you both. Then note down your body language, voice, pauses, questions used and consider how the use of your interpersonal skills assisted or hindered the conversation.

This activity is not easy and may feel a little contrived. Do not worry if you found it hard or were constrained because you were concentrating on your skills and the way you presented. It is important to begin this process of awareness-raising in a safe context before you work with service users.

Let us briefly set Rebecca, Melissa and Irene in the context of systems thinking and the use of interpersonal skills.

CASE STUDY

In simple terms we can see that the three people involved – Rebecca, Melissa and Irene – interact together and influence each other. They are also sub-systems or elements of a wider family system that interacts with social workers, health visitors, Melissa's boyfriend and no doubt with other families. The importance of this way of thinking is to recognise that Rebecca's care is not the concern of just her immediate family and that there is a range of influences on a person's life.

In undertaking the initial assessment and negotiating the plan, Mandy, Rebecca's social worker, used her skills to set everyone at ease, to listen to Melissa, Irene and others, to summarise, check and reproduce what was said. This took time and depended on developing a relationship that had clear boundaries: Mandy explained the purpose of the work, what could be confidential and what could not be. She then negotiated with the family a plan to meet Rebecca's needs. This negotiation needed to be joint and allow everyone involved to contribute in their own way. Any assessment, plan, intervention or review will be influenced by the quality of the social worker's interpersonal skills.

Empirical intervention models

As we have seen throughout this book, there is an ongoing debate concerning our interpretation of social work as either an 'art' or a 'science'. There are many cross-over points between the two arguments. In this section you will be introduced to models that are empirically based, that is, the outcomes and effects can be observed and measured and an inference made as to their impact on situations. However, these models require skill and artistry to be effective and, as we shall see, they acknowledge the fluidity and dynamic aspects of service user situations. Whilst you will be introduced to these models using a children and families perspective, the interventions can be transferred to other social work situations and service user groups. Indeed, it may be useful to spend time thinking how you might use these models with Gladys.

Task-centred practice

In working directly with Melissa, Mandy used a task-centred approach to achieving the goals that were made clear by the plan. The task-centred approach is an extremely practical model for social work. It suggests that beneficial and desired changes can be achieved by working in partnership with service users to resolve other areas of concern. Whilst partnership is stressed, task-centred practice can be used with people who do not wish to work with you and those whose capacity to make agreements is limited because it centres on goals that are negotiated and agreed between service users and social workers. It is, therefore, a useful model to employ as part of wider social work intervention. The emphasis is upon small, achievable targets and goals and can involve individuals, whole families or wider groups in the selection, prioritising and work towards the achievement of these. It is helpful to view task centred practice as a set of building blocks (Marsh and Doel, 2005) or as a series climbed by agreement between the social worker and service users as seen below.

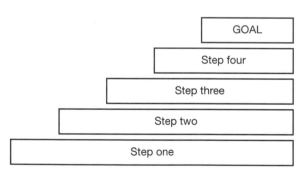

A step approach to achieving goals

Although the originators of the approach suggested that task-centred work was simply a pragmatic way of working that was not based on any underlying theory, this is not the case (Reid and Epstein, 1972; Reid, 1978). Task-centred work is associated with problem-solving and behavioural approaches to social work (Doel, 2002; Gambrill, 1994; Parker and Penhale, 1998). The successful accomplishment of tasks rewards people and motivates them to try to act in other areas of their lives. Whatever the theory underlying task-centred practice, however, it is about purposeful actions. The work undertaken is time-limited, structured and problem-focused. It represents an active collaboration between practitioner and service user.

Task-centred practice has been adopted by many social workers and by agencies. Its simple sequencing of steps building to agreed goals fits with the tasks demanded by policies and procedures associated with contemporary social work. Its popularity also owes a great deal to the positive features which characterise it:

- the aims and purpose are clear and specific;
- a contractual agreement is negotiated between workers and service users;
- task-centred practice concentrates upon achievable goals;
- it is time-limited;
- it is task-oriented, structured and sequential;
- it is effective and measurable.

RESEARCH SUMMARY

Development of the task-centred model

The model first developed in North America in the 1960s as a response to growing dissatisfaction with open-ended psychodynamic approaches to social work and an increasing emphasis on the participation of service users. Alongside this, there was a search for effective and economically efficient models of social work intervention.

In 1969, Reid and Shyne conducted an experiment that marked the development of the specific interventive technique of task-centred practice. The relative merits of short-term and extended social work practice were compared. The idea of brief practice was a novel concept for most social workers at this time and therefore a particular intervention strategy was developed, consisting of four stages.

1. Focus on the key aspect of the problem, issue or area of concern.

2. Open, honest and explicit collaboration.

3. A review of the progress made towards achieving goals and objectives.

4. An emphasis on generalising learning for the future.

The findings of this research indicated that short-term focused interventions led to more progress during the intervention and that accrued benefits were just as durable six months after the intervention as longer-term approaches.

Developing on from this work, Reid and Epstein (1972) developed task-centred practice. From their research they presented a seven-point typology of problems for which task-centred work may be effective:

- *interpersonal conflict;*
- *dissatisfaction in social relations;*
- *relations with formal organisations;*
- *role performance;*

RESEARCH SUMMARY

- *social transition;*

- *reactive emotional distress;*

- *inadequate resources*

In a later work, however, Reid (1978) extended this typology to include the catch-all of any other psychological or behavioural problem not specified in the original typology but fitting the general principles of task-centred practice.

A model for practice

There is a general agreement on the stages and processes involved in task-centred work. Marsh and Doel (2005) breakdown task-centred practice into 13 elements:

- mandate

- problems and goals

- goals

- exploring problems

- focusing problems

- refining goals

- time limits

- the recorded agreement

- tasks and the task role

- task development

- review

- ending and evaluating

- continuing.

These are more often conflated within core stages such as within the following four-stage approach:

- developing a focus on the problem;

- reaching agreement: goals and contracts;

- developing goals into manageable tasks;

- ending and reviewing the work.

Problem-solving is central to the requirements of the new degree and explicitly mentioned in the subject benchmarks. This makes task-centred practice a particularly valuable model for practice. The exploration, identification, specification and prioritisation of a problem to work upon is fundamental to the model. All models debate at some point the formulation of an agreement between service users and practitioners. There is considerable debate, however, whether this agreement should be written or remain verbal. The action focus is central to the model and process. This includes planning and agreeing tasks, specifying roles and responsibilities, completing agreed tasks, reviewing achievements and modifying planning. Although an element of review is included at each stage the final session is devoted to an overall review of the accomplishments of the service user. We shall now explore this model in greater detail applying it to the case of Rebecca and Melissa.

Developing a focus on the problem

The initial assessment focuses on the reasons for social work involvement, the wants and wishes of the service users and begins to create a sharper focus to the work. We have seen in Chapter 1 that assessments often take a funnel-like approach to problem specification; the problem gradually becoming more specific and focused. The use of the term 'problem' may be seen as controversial. Stress on the strengths of service users is recognised as increasingly important and talking about 'problems' may be construed as negative and to some extent 'pathological'. However, it is important to remember that service users will often describe elements of their lives and situations as problematic and we must listen to these perceptions. It would be arrogant to suggest their problems are simply 'solution opportunities'! It is also the case that by working with you as a social worker on identifying areas of life for change service users are demonstrating strengths and capacity for change.

In task-centred practice, the identification of problems is a joint venture in which service users are encouraged to describe problems or issues as they see them. These are then placed in some kind of rank order. Social workers check their understanding and construct an initial problem profile with service users and others to gain corroborative information. At this stage agreement can be reached on the priority area to be worked upon.

Once the range of problems has been prioritised a target problem can be chosen and described in detail. The process is collaborative at all stages and encourages the active involvement of service users.

In the assessment of Melissa, Rebecca and Irene you will recall that three issues were highlighted for work. These consisted of a break from caring, joining a young mum's group and work on Melissa and Irene's relationship. Two of these were seen as problems that Melissa wanted to overcome, whilst attending the young mums' group was something she wanted to try.

In the assessment process and in constructing a plan the social worker was working with Melissa to prioritise problems and to identify targets for change.

Reaching agreement: goals and contracts

The second stage of task-centred work concerns reaching an agreement about goals and working together to achieve them. The selection of goals advances on the ranking of problems and issues to change in priority order. The key issue in reaching agreement about goals is to ensure that the service user leads the process. The task of the social worker is to keep the service user on track and to ensure that goals identified are achievable and realistic. Doel (1994) identifies three important factors that need to be considered when you are working with service users to define and agree upon goals.

These comprise:

- checking out that the goal is really what the person wants to achieve as this will increase motivation to work towards it;

- making sure that goals are feasible and achievable;

- determining whether the goal is acceptable to agency policy and values.

Once a goal is identified and agreed, it is important to agree on a course of action to achieve it. An important way of recording this agreement is to negotiate a written agreement specifying exactly what will be done, who will do what, and when and how they will do it. There is a debate as to whether the agreement between service users and practitioners should be written or should remain oral. Whilst oral agreements can be less frightening and imposing, and are necessary where a person cannot read, a written contract or agreement adds to specificity, and can be referred to at a later date if a dispute over tasks or responsibilities arises. They can be extremely useful in establishing clear parameters for work where remembering is difficult or where there are many people involved.

The agreement reached with Melissa identified an overall goal or objective of giving *the best possible start in life for Rebecca*. This was not specific and needed to be discussed further to identify what would help achieve this broad objective in Melissa's view. The written agreement and plan added a degree of clarity to the process. Whilst Melissa and her mother were quite literate it is important to consider difficulties with understanding written documents, and to ensure that alternative formats are available where appropriate. For instance, the use of tape recorded agreements may help where people have difficulty reading or an interpreter may help where English is not spoken or a second language.

Developing goals into manageable tasks

Planned tasks must be explicit, practicable for service users to undertake outside of formal sessions and mutually agreed. Payne (2005) identifies two basic types of task:

- general tasks which set out the agency's intervention and work policy;

- operational tasks which define exactly what will be done to achieve the goals that are set.

Tasks may involve a single action or a set of smaller actions that join together. They may be set for the service user to complete alone, or the service user may complete one task whilst the social worker or another involved person does something else. Tasks may also be shared. However, it is important to note that tasks are individual to the specific situation in which they have been developed. At this point a more specific and task-focused agreement can be negotiated. An example is shown in respect of Melissa.

The general tasks for Melissa were detailed in the plan. However, Mandy worked with Melissa to consider a more detailed set of steps to integrate her into the young mums' group. To begin the process, Mandy arranged a meeting between June Bridge, the health visitor, Melissa and herself. This meeting was convened to consider the process needed to ease Melissa into the group.

Melissa had become keen on attending because of the support she would gain. She was, however, nervous about joining and meeting new people. She also found it more difficult to get up in the morning as Rebecca was not sleeping well in the night. Melissa agreed to:

- purchase an alarm clock;

- meet June Bridge on Thursday at 9 a.m.;

- be taken by June to the group and to stay for one hour.

This would be reviewed by June, Melissa and Mandy on the Monday following the session. It was also agreed that if this plan had worked well Melissa would meet June at the group on the following Thursday and stay for the morning. Subsequently, Melissa would attend the group on Tuesdays and Thursdays. This would be reviewed weekly for four weeks by Mandy and Melissa.

It is important to highlight again the need for clarity, specificity and simplicity when constructing the tasks. It can be helpful to think 'If I were to be abducted by aliens and could not get to work, would my colleagues understand the tasks in the same way as I do?' It is crucial for the service user to have the same understanding as yourself and this makes great demands on how you use and develop your interpersonal skills.

The social work role is now directed towards facilitating the achievement of the agreed tasks by the service user. As the intervention process proceeds, the tasks may be revised and made more specific and clear if this becomes necessary. This allows progress to be measured and the intervention to be altered to achieve maximum gain for the service user. The social work role, your 'tasks' and the intensity of involvement depend upon the agreement, the strengths and capacity of the service user and others who may help with the programme. This flexibility allows the model to be used with a wide range of people in many situations.

At each session the social worker and service should review the achievements made. This provides a useful starting point for each session and looks at strengths and obstacles or barriers to be overcome. Doel (1994) points out that service users' motivation may wane over time and, as a result, tasks may remain unaccomplished. If social workers identify this they may be able to renegotiate with service users and, if necessary, modify the goals. It was important for Mandy to support and encourage Melissa's attendance when she was getting up and going to the group on her own. It must be remembered that sometimes the goals negotiated are either not the ones the service user really wants to achieve or they are not realistic and achievable. Progress may be diverted off course, however, by a range of other factors affecting the lives of service users. There needs to be a degree of flexibility to adapt the process where necessary. It is sometimes helpful to involve carers and other involved people to assist in goal achievement. This may encourage perseverance and, if the contract is written, can help to keep a focus on the agreed tasks and the goals sought.

Ending and reviewing the work

It is important that the time-limited nature of the intervention is mentioned at the outset to the intervention and that a planned end to the work is emphasised. This clear focus can keep service users 'on track' and encourage motivation to achieve agreed goals. The ending phase is part of the agreement to work together and is therefore undertaken collaboratively between client and worker. In respect of Melissa social work support was continuing but the specific agreement to introduce her to the young mums' group was time-limited. She was eased into the group at which point the health visitor withdrew. The social work involvement continued whilst she became established and after four weeks the focus of this work shifted to the other objectives identified in the plan.

It may happen, however, that no matter how carefully planned the intervention has been, the service user does not wish to end contact even if goals have been achieved. This may sometimes highlight a new and different need for work and this can be discussed as and when appropriate. When the agreed goal has not been achieved by the end of the planned sessions more time may be negotiated if it is felt this will help service users to reach the goals (Doel, 1994). It may also be the case that the task-centred work is part of a wider involvement between social work and service user. In this case the negotiated and planned ending of a piece of work may represent a staging post or milestone in gaining skills and assist closure of the case in the future. The process is flexible and made individual to the situation in which the work takes place.

Throughout the four key stages involved in task-centred practice it is important to be both systematic in what is undertaken and flexible in response to changing needs. Being systematic keeps the service user focused on the task in hand, but you need to be flexible enough to acknowledge other concerns and factors in the service user's life. This model of intervention fits the practical emphasis of the new degree, the problem-solving focus and the need to demonstrate effectiveness. It also fits many agency approaches. We will now turn to a more complex model that is also grounded in effectiveness.

Cognitive behavioural approaches to practice

Cognitive behavioural approaches to practice have had, at times, a negative press over the years. This is partly due to a misunderstanding of the methods and processes involved. It has been suggested that giving rewards for good behaviour is tantamount to bribery, that feelings are ignored, that past experiences are not taken into account and that cognitive behavioural approaches reduce human actions to component parts in a way that fails to acknowledge the whole person. By far the most common criticism of cognitive behavioural approaches comes from those practitioners who base their views on misguided bad practice and programmes that use unethical techniques such as punishments and aversive methods.

However, we all engage in behaviour. Behaviours are observable and behavioural actions represent a response to, within, on, or as part of the wider social environment in which we live. The first use of behavioural approaches only considered observable behaviours. However, recently, it was recognised that behaviours are closely linked with thoughts about how we ought to act in particular situations and under particular circumstances. Thoughts often relate to our prior experiences and result from our daily 'experiments' or interactions with the world around us. Behaviour is now acknowledged to have a thinking or cognitive element to it. As a result, the term cognitive behavioural has been adopted as an umbrella term for behavioural and cognitive approaches to practice.

In simple terms, cognitive behavioural approaches involve the systematic alteration of behaviours or thoughts by increasing, decreasing or maintaining them. A cognitive behavioural intervention involves altering the setting in which the behaviour occurs, or its triggers, cues and prompts and its consequences. Increasing behaviours that are agreed by social workers and service users or carers to be constructive and positive for that person and reducing the occurrence of behaviours that are agreed to be unhelpful or negative represent the primary aims of cognitive behavioural programmes. This objective of changing behaviours has sparked criticism that such interventions are directive, manipulative and simply uphold socially acceptable patterns of behaviour. If this were the case it would clearly come into conflict with the range of different ways of behaving across cultures, social groups and within families and would be liable to ignore the needs of individuals. Fortunately, this criticism is not valid as cognitive behavioural intervention is subject to the same values and ethics of any other intervention programme in social work and, to be effective, must have the active agreement and involvement of service users.

Cognitive behavioural approaches are based on the idea that if behaviour is learnt then it can be unlearnt, or new behaviours can be learnt to replace less useful ones. It is the concern of people using these approaches to widen the range of possible responses that an individual can make to their environment and to be able to change it, and not to limit, direct and determine people's actions. In this sense it is a highly ethical approach that accords with the codes of ethics of social care professional bodies (British Association of Social Workers, 2002; GSCC, 2002).

A number of key theories explaining the ways in which we learn to behave have been developed. Four of these models are commonly used in social work practice:

- respondent or classical conditioning;

- operant or instrumental conditioning;

- modelling, imitative or vicarious learning;

- cognitive-behavioural theories.

Respondent and operant conditioning models are concerned with what can be seen whilst modelling concerns a person's interpretation of what another person does and cognitive behavioural approaches are related to the ways in which thoughts lead to certain consequences or actions. In this section of the chapter we will concentrate on the first two models since they are well known and acknowledged to be useful within important areas of social work practice. These models will be explored in respect of Rebecca and Melissa although they can be applied with equal effectiveness in adult social work. As you develop your knowledge and skills you may wish to develop your understanding of the other models. (A good place to start would be to consult Cigno, 2002; Cigno and Bourn, 1998; Parker and Randall, 1997; Sheldon, 1995.) An outline of respondent and operant conditioning models follows.

Respondent or classical conditioning
In this theory, behaviours are prompted or triggered by association with a certain event or stimulus. For instance, being asked to give an oral presentation for your course work may lead to your palms sweating, a dry throat and nausea. The same response may also occur when the initial prompt, being asked to give an oral presentation, is associated or paired with a second event or stimulus. Let us say that in this instance the oral presentation is to be assessed. When next asked to complete a piece of assessed casework, but no oral presentation, the same response occurs again. This is known as respondent conditioning because the behaviour is considered to be a response to the stimuli eliciting it.

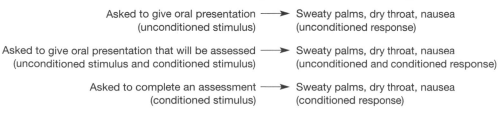

A respondent conditioning model

Social workers using a respondent conditioning approach might attempt to replace the anxiety response by pairing the stimulus with something that would trigger more comfortable and positive reactions, perhaps associating lying on a sun-soaked beach with just enough of a breeze to keep you cool with being asked to give an oral presentation. The responses – positive and negative – would then compete and hopefully the positive response would begin to replace the negative one. Social workers might also look at adapting the response. They may teach you to relax your muscles and to breathe slowly and deeply. After learning these skills the social worker may gradually introduce the idea of undertaking an oral presentation, and you may be able to bring up the relaxed response when presented with the request to give an oral presentation. These two responses compete and, hopefully, being able to relax when faced with an initially anxiety-provoking stimulus will help you to adapt the response and cope much better with this situation.

Operant or instrumental conditioning

Respondent conditioning theory is quite a simple way of describing the ways in which we learn. Another theory of learning that is similar to respondent conditioning is operant learning theory. Rather than a response or behaviour being triggered or prompted by a situation or event, this theory states that behaviours are learnt and repeated because of the consequences immediately following their expression. The strength, frequency and type of these consequences greatly influence any future expression of the preceding behaviour.

Specific settings or behaviours do not automatically elicit operant behaviour, but they are important as they provide cues for the kind of behaviour that is likely to result in gaining the reward or consequence that is desired. These cues are known as antecedent stimuli. If a social worker learns what signals or cues precede behaviour, intervention can be directed at altering them. However, social workers are also likely to want to help service users change the consequences that make the behaviour that is targeted for change likely to happen.

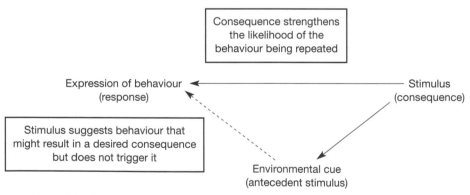

Operant learning theory

Using theories of learning

Let us return to the case of Rebecca and Melissa three years forward in time to see how these models of learning can help in social work practice. In order to begin to alter behaviour, social workers will work alongside service users and carers to identify patterns that trigger or reinforce the behaviour by rewarding it. This demands a more focused and specific assessment relating directly to an identified and agreed target behaviour. This might come from the wider assessment process and the negotiations that take place. The important point to note is that the target behaviour is more likely to be changed if it is identified and agreed by the service user and social worker. Not only is this important in meeting the ethical demands of social work but also in achieving success in the intervention. The target of the intervention must be clearly and explicitly specified. This is not easy to achieve and you will benefit from practice in describing behaviours in clear, specific and commonly understandable ways.

A cognitive behavioural assessment concerns who does what, where, when, how often and with whom. Sticking to these questions creates focus, clarity and specificity.

CASE STUDY

Rebecca is nearly 4 years old. Melissa is a single parent again following the break up of her relationship two years ago. Recently, Melissa has been referred to the social work team because of 'shouting and screaming' at her daughter. Melissa was pleased with the prospect of support because of her previous involvement with social services but embarrassed and defensive because of the nature of the referral.

She told David, the social worker, that Rebecca was 'too much of a handful and will never do as she's told.' Melissa agreed that she was finding it difficult to control Rebecca and was shouting a lot. This gave David some information but it remained broad and non-specific. He used a series of 'who, what, where, when and how' questions to create focus, explaining to Melissa that they could work together to create a clear understanding of the situation and then seek alternatives.

The main times that Melissa became cross was at Rebecca's bedtime. Rebecca was very active and wanted to play games, have drinks and be read stories continually. The usual pattern was that after eating at about 5.30 p.m. Melissa would wash the dishes until she gave in to Rebecca's requests for a story – her favourite at the moment being The tiger who came to tea. *After the story, Rebecca would ask to play a game – generally 'snap' or 'pairs'. This would, Melissa said, continue until bedtime and then Rebecca would ask for a drink or a biscuit. On further exploration, David was told that although Melissa tried to take some time out the 'constant nagging' led to her giving in and responding to her requests. When Melissa felt that Rebecca was delaying her bedtime she would 'snap' and shout.*

David had more information to work with now and asked 'what is it that you would most like to change?' Melissa brought up two things: she would like Rebecca to give her some free time in the evening and she would like to be able to stop shouting at Rebecca. A target time of 30 minutes divided into two 15 minute slots was agreed.

David needed to work with Melissa and Rebecca to record the frequency of these behaviours and to identify any patterns that might be amenable to change. In order to do this he needed to be very precise about what the behaviours or targets were. They decided on 'shouting at Rebecca' and 'sitting down with a cup of tea' as this characterised her attempts at free time. David explained carefully the information to be recorded and checked with Melissa that she was able to undertake this. It can be the case that insufficient attention is paid to this part of the process and service users either do not complete the recording or record something different to what the social worker expected. Feeling confident that she was able to record the situation, David suggested that she keep two questions in mind:

CASE STUDY *continued*

1. What happens when you shout at Rebecca?

2. What happens when you take time away from Rebecca in the evening?

Melissa was asked to complete two charts detailing exactly what happend before the tar-geted behaviour, when, where, in what ways, and with whom and what happened immediately following the behaviour. He asked Melissa to collect this information over the course of the week and to do so as soon after the event as possible so it was not lost or 'reinterpreted'. Typical examples of the recordings follow:

	Antecedent	Behaviour (agreed behaviour: shouting at Rebecca)	Consequence
Date/time	Called Rebecca for bed, she asked me to play one more game with her, agreed if she would come to bed immediately after. Rebecca then asked for a drink	Shouted at Rebecca	I felt guilty and gave her a drink and a cuddle

	Antecedent/situation	Behaviour	Consequence
Date/time	Sat down to drink a cup of tea	Rebecca asked me to play snap five times	Played snap whilst drinking tea

'ABC' charts for Rebecca and Melissa.

David was able to explore with Melissa how the problems were likely to be maintained. It appeared over the course of the week that Melissa shouted at Rebecca when she 'stalled for time' in going to bed, and that whilst this acted as a trigger to Melissa, she was inad-vertently making Rebecca's delaying tactics more likely by often doing what she had asked for in the first place. It seemed also to be the case that Melissa reinforced Rebecca's requests for her to play by eventually agreeing to play with her. It is important when look-ing at patterns like these not to be accusatory or to blame people for 'causing' problems. This needs to be handled sensitively and explaining the social ways in which we learn may help. David set out in visual form the pattern of occurrences.

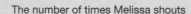
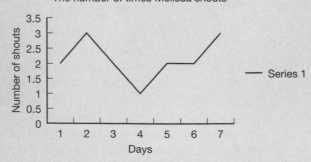

The number of times Melissa shouts

— Series 1

A visual display of the number of times Melissa shouts

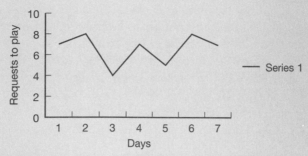

Requests to play with Rebecca

They discussed what they might do to change the situation and David asked Melissa to bring Rebecca into this discussion then she would be aware of the plans. It is important to involve all people who may be affected by the programme. It is courteous and shows respect taking into account age and understanding. They agreed to plan in to the evenings two 15-minute breaks during which Melissa would not play with Rebecca but after which she would be given the choice of what to do. It was also agreed to help Melissa to learn to relax and to use these techniques when feeling fraught. These plans drew on operant and respondent conditioning and considered manipulating triggers and consequences that seemed to be maintaining these situations.

Melissa would tell Rebecca five minutes before her break that it would be happening. Then she would mention it again as she went to spend time on her own. Rebecca agreed to play on her own and would be able to choose the next game if she did not disturb Melissa during this time. Melissa agreed to explain firmly and calmly that she was having a break if Rebecca asked her for something. She was not to give in. Importantly, David explained to Melissa that often behaviour that you wish to change gets worse for a time before gradually reducing and that this can be a difficult time but she would succeed if she persevered. They agreed to monitor and record this situation for a week using the same forms as before, and David again prepared a visual display of the changes.

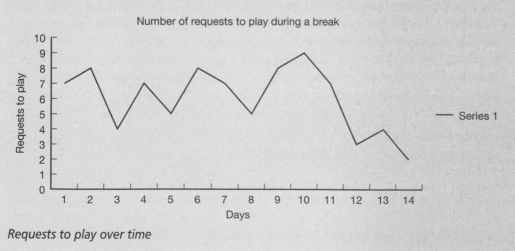

Requests to play over time

Melissa was heartened to see this working and said she felt much calmer. However, she was still concerned about shouting at Rebecca, although she was not giving in to her requests at bedtime. David encouraged her to keep a firm approach and also taught her deep muscle relaxation, recognising how each muscle felt when tense and relaxed, and asked her to practise this when faced with a challenge. Melissa tried this over the following week, especially when she felt she was about to shout at Rebecca. She recorded the number of times she shouted and also how she felt. This information helped Melissa to see the positive changes and developments made over time.

Cognitive behavioural approaches are useful and effective but they can be complex and care must be taken over each part of the process, especially in respect of including service users in the planning and implementation of the work. It must also be remembered that if a behaviour is to change by replacing the consequence by a different one, this must be recognised by the individual as important and stronger than the consequence they already gain from behaving in the way you and they wish to change. Choosing something to reinforce a new behaviour is an activity that is complex and open to failure if it is not done in full participation with service users. Imagine a situation in which a friend wanted to help you alter one of your behaviours but this behaviour made you very popular with other friends. If your friend chose to replace the popularity you gained from behaving in this way with a chance to see a football match, but you did not enjoy football, it would be unlikely to alter your behaviour!

Intervening with adults; some models

Cognitive behavioural programmes can be used with adults as well as with children and families. However, we turn now to consider interventions that can be usefully applied when working with older people within a care management and single assessment process. Particularly we refer to crisis intervention drawing on some psychodynamic theories and also networking skills and advocacy. Older people do not have a monopoly on these interventions, and indeed they are equally appropriate for other service user groups. Nonetheless, we describe them here in order to build your knowledge and understanding so that, when we look at the developing case of Gladys Beaumont, you are familiar with the interventions. Indeed, we hope that you will be able to extrapolate from the information provided in order to work out how you think the hospital based care manager, Sarah Jacobs, should have worked with Gladys Beaumont whilst she was on the surgical ward.

Crisis theory and crisis intervention

First we look at the development of crisis theory and crisis intervention and also at the practical application of crisis intervention in social work situations. We shall then go on to consider this intervention in relation to the case of Gladys Beaumont. This is an appropriate approach to use with Gladys, given the shock and trauma she felt when she learned that her leg was to be amputated, and that her life was at some considerable risk. For a fuller explanation of crisis intervention we suggest you read Chapter 4 in Parker and Penhale's (1998, pages 51–70) *Forgotten people* on which much of this section is based.

Let us consider some definitions which may help to unpack the concept. Crises are described as time-limited periods of psychological distress that people need to overcome but cannot do so using tried and tested methods of coping (Caplan, 1961; Roberts, 1991).

Definitions of what constitutes a crisis situation are to some extent in the perception of the beholder. Further, we need to conceptualise crisis in a fluid and dynamic sense. Its interpretation does not rest upon a particular event or situation or even a particular response. Rather the individual's perception of, for example, powerlessness, lack of control and psychological distress located within a particular contextual environment, provides meaning. Whatever the event or situation triggering the crisis, it seems that there are certain key features involved in the experience of crises. Parry (1990, page 15) suggests that these comprise:

- a precipitating event or the result of long-term stress;

- individually experienced distress;

- a sense of loss, danger to the self or humiliation;

- feelings of being out of control of the situation;

- events which may be unexpected;

- disruption in usual patterns and routines;

- the future is uncertain; and

- distress continues over time, although this is limited.

Crises can be *accidental* – a reaction to unexpected traumatic events – or *developmental* – a reaction to a life transition. Both types are potentially important when considering reactions to bereavement and when dealing with life-threatening illness, such as that experienced by Gladys Beaumont. The idea of crisis representing a turning point that presents problems for the individual that he or she cannot solve without external help is helpful (Aguilera and Messick, 1974; 1982). We shall return to these ideas when illustrating our complex case.

A particular crisis event is likely to influence a particular social system in a unique way which in turn influences and is influenced by participating sub-systems and its environment. The use of systems theory may allow a social worker/care manager to conceptualise the wider conflicting processes impinging upon a particular crisis situation. In the case of Gladys Beaumont we see how her immediate support system and networks are affected as a result of her personal and health crises.

The development of crisis theory

Crisis theory and crisis intervention have a long history of development. Roberts (1991) draws on thinking from 400BC, when referring to Hippocrates' understanding of the importance of crises in medicine and health. Current understanding is informed predominantly by American psychiatry. The conceptual and theoretical origins have arisen from varied sources, but primarily from psychoanalytic thinking and the principle of causality that holds that present behaviour needs to be understood in terms of life history and past experiences. Put simply, people normally cope better with crises if they have dealt effectively with other crises in their lives, conversely they cope less well if they have unresolved past problems. The theoretical base has developed in sophistication, especially following Lindemann's (1944) study of grief reactions of survivors and relatives after a night-club fire in Coconut Grove, Boston. Lindemann and colleagues found that many individuals experiencing acute grief shared five related reactions as follows:

1. *Somatic distress (physical sensations such as stomach complaints or headaches).*

2. *Preoccupation with the image of the deceased.*

3. *Guilt.*

4. *Hostile reactions.*

5. *Loss of patterns of conduct.*

Also, they found that the duration of the reaction appeared to be dependent upon the success of the grief work. Lindemann found that people needed encouragement to mourn and to adjust to the changed environment.

The development of crisis theory is underpinned by a range of different and complex theories which we will not explore in detail here. They include the following.

- Erikson's (1950) developmental psychology, and Hartmann's (1958) ego psychology. Within this framework, personal development is seen as the result of a series of crises through which we move, that result from adapting to attachment and loss within normal human growth and development.

- Drawing on Parkes' (1972) work, Payne (2005) explains that when a person has a significant loss, they may 'regress to childhood experiences of stress due to loss' (page 77). Similarly, Pincus' (1976) work illustrates the point that in their reaction to death, family members may reveal hidden and high levels of unresolved feelings about former relationships.

- Person-centred approaches (Rogers, 1961) and gestalt therapy (Perls, Hefferline and Goodman, 1973) have also influenced the development of crisis intervention. These therapies focus on the 'here and now' and on the personal growth opportunities that crisis work creates (see Parker, 2007b).

Crisis intervention – a time of opportunity

A crisis presents an opportunity for social workers to influence positively the coping capacities of others. Conversely, crisis intervention if handled inappropriately may also distort reality and lead to maladaptive coping strategies. It is at this time when a person's defences are lowered, that they are more likely to be motivated and willing to change, that practical application of crisis theory is effective (see work by Rapoport, 1970; Golan, 1978; Baldwin, 1979; Aguilera and Messick, 1982; Olsen, 1984; Gilbar, 1991; O'Hagan, 1991 and Edlis, 1993). Given our understanding of crises as time-limited and potentially constructive periods of opportunity, it is important to determine with the service user what constitutes a successful resolution to them and to work towards clearly defined goals.

The multiple applications of crisis theory and intervention

Crisis intervention has been used with positive results in many settings and with many different service user groups, not only with people who are bereaved or diagnosed with life-threatening illnesses, such as that experienced by Gladys Beaumont. These include suicide, mental health issues (Roberts,1995), domestic violence; rape crisis (Edlis, 1993); children and families (O'Hagan, 1991).

Crisis intervention and social work

Most referrals to social workers are made at points of crisis. The initial assessment and intervention, including the provision of practical help, support and reassurance, advice and further referral when appropriate can, as seen in the context of crisis theory, influence the outcome of that situation for good or ill. All social work skills must be employed towards achieving a constructive resolution of the crisis. For example, skills such as advocacy, bargaining, negotiation, use of empathy and appropriate challenging are drawn on. Service users are generally part of larger living systems, and changes effected within the group of family and friends with whom they live, are close and significant may in some ways resolve a crisis situation. It is important to decide who is in crisis. The following checklist sets out some of the questions that are useful to ask when working with crises.

CHECKLIST

Crisis intervention flow diagram (source Parker, 1992, page 55)
1. Determine whether the referral situation constitutes a crisis.

2. Identify for whom this is a crisis.

3. Agree the wants, wishes and needs of the significant participants.

4. Check:

    i. legal and statutory obligations;

    ii. availability of local resources and services;

    iii. values – personal, professional, service user.

---

5. *Negotiate an initial working agreement.*

6. *Co-ordinate services and implement initial plan of care.*

7. *Review, renegotiate and formulate care plan.*

Crisis intervention provides a unique opportunity to work towards constructive change, to intervene in order to optimise social functioning and enable choice, and participation and to provide appropriate services. Given the possibilities for change, intervening in crises offers the practitioner a chance to build trust, rapport and work in partnership with service users to honour the values common to social work and within the legislation – that individual choice should be respected and maximised and that people should be enabled to live as independent a life as possible.

CASE STUDY

Gladys Beaumont and crisis intervention

Gladys' key nurse, Jane Sykes, went out of her way to talk to Sarah Jacobs, the care manager attached to the surgical ward. She had noticed that Gladys was very upset following her operation for a below the knee amputation. Gladys was not sleeping well and barely eating. She seldom spoke and several fellow patients and the night staff had said that she could be heard sobbing throughout the night; sometimes she would cry out for her mother. It is normal for people to be upset and grieve the loss of a limb, but Gladys' response seemed more severe and Jane feared that she was 'turning her head to the wall'. The stump was not healing and Jane was of the view that something was stopping the healing process. She had alerted Sarah since she knew that her colleague had years of experience in such matters and was a skilled practitioner.

Sarah approached Gladys tentatively. She 'felt her way' into what was at first a stilted conversation and sought Gladys' agreement to move into a quiet room off the ward. Gladys passively agreed, her reluctance stemmed from her heavy heart; she had completely forgotten her earlier, negative experience of social services.

Even though Gladys knew that the 'small talk' in which they started to engage was to help put her at her ease, she felt Sarah to be sensitive and caring. After a short while, Sarah encouraged Gladys to talk about the events leading to the hospital admission and Gladys responded, in a flat monotone voice. Finding a receptive audience, Gladys responded to Sarah's gentle prompts and she proceeded to describe what had happened to her in hospital and subsequently. Gladys began to cry softly when describing her conversation with the surgeon. He had told her quite forthrightly that if she did not agree to the operation then her life would be in danger and that she needed to 'stabilise her diabetes' and take active steps to address her high blood pressure, if not he would be seeing her again 'in a matter of months for a second amputation.' Gladys broke down at this point and Sarah held her hand and encouraged her to express her feelings fully. Gladys said that she did not want to die, that she was ashamed of the way she had ignored her health and 'let herself go'. Sarah told Gladys that she was in a state of shock and crisis in reaction to these traumatic events and that this was very normal. Sarah spent time listening to Gladys repeat the story and bring herself to a state where she seemed less agitated. Before she left she had gained Gladys' agreement that they should work together to 'talk about her problems and take some action.'

Sarah's initial assessment was that Gladys was in a state of crisis and that brief therapy in the form of crisis intervention could be the way forward. She knew that if she were to work with Gladys then she would need to see her again soon to start the work which would be focused and time-limited, not least due to the competing priorities of Sarah's other commitments in her role as care manager attached to a busy surgical ward. She knew that she would have to negotiate some extra time, with her line manager, to spend on this case.

The following day Sarah and Gladys met again. This time Gladys was both apprehensive and yet ready to talk about the feelings that the trauma had triggered. She said she could not stop herself going over in her mind all the past hurts. She kept thinking of her mother with whom she had been very close and who died unexpectedly when she was in her mid-fifties. At that time Gladys was married and was looking after her husband who was seriously ill. She felt unable to spend the time she wanted with her mother and was not there at her death. Her husband and her mother died within two weeks of each other, and yet it was the loss of her mother that continues to grieve her. She recalled that she never said goodbye to her mother, nor had she told her heartfelt and important things. Gladys wanted to know why this was troubling her now and why her whole situation seemed to overwhelm her.

Although Sarah knew a great deal about crisis intervention she was sensitive not to resort to 'jargon' or too much theory. She explained that it was common that feelings of loss in one area, such as the loss of a limb, may trigger similar feelings in another that remained unresolved. Gladys responded to this point and said that it helped her heavy heart just to talk. Sarah said there were no miracle cures and that Gladys' crisis could go one of two ways; she could continue to be overwhelmed by it and this was a danger, or alternatively, she could take the opportunity to learn new ways of coping in both her internal emotional life and her external social life. Sarah emphasised that the power was with Gladys; it was her choice to decide what she now wanted from life. Sarah said that she would make no assumptions or judgements about the outcome, other than that both had to be clear what they were aiming for and what would constitute a successful resolution. She also commented that it was not entirely up to Gladys, other people whom Gladys valued in the community had a part to play, as did the health and social care services. In this way Sarah began to negotiate and construct an initial agreement.

Gladys said that she wanted her life back, but not the old life. Not the passive life when she stayed alone at home waiting for the few visitors to arrive. Rather she recognised that she had had in her terms a near death experience and that life was short and precious; she no longer could take being alive for granted. She felt self-conscious about her weight and about a life style which had helped to reinforce her health problems. She felt humbled by the support and kindness shown by her neighbour, for whom she had little time in the past and particularly given the difficulties with the leylandii hedge which she had perpetuated. She had been surprised that the local church had organised a rota so that people she hardly knew from the village had taken it in turn to visit. She had expected her niece to visit more often but in her new heightened state of awareness, she could see that she had never taken an interest in her niece's life so why should she show interest in her now? Whilst recognising her physical disabilities and uncertainties about her rehabilitation, Gladys firmly wanted to be more involved in her community; play bridge, watch the bowling in the park, visit the local garden centres, perhaps attend a keep fit class. But above all she wanted to have better relationships with those people whom she had kept 'at arm's length'. Gladys agreed that life was going to be hard living alone at home but she now saw the positives from being in the same locality where she grew up and also knowing her way around. She saw her former desire to move to the Isle of Wight for what it was – a form of escapism and avoidance from facing up to her less than fulfilling life. Now she was determined to join in things and 'get a life'.

ACTIVITY 4.2

In the ten days in which Gladys is confined to her hospital bed what do you think is achievable and could be written into a working agreement which will help Gladys to overcome this crisis? Keep the plan simple, feasible and 'doable'. Stay with Gladys' informal life and the known links. (The health and social care plan that involves her physical and social rehabilitation are dealt with in other chapters, although her wishes as expressed here will become part of that plan.) Perhaps it may help Gladys if she wrote a letter to her dead mother expressing how she felt about her. What do you think she would write in such a letter?

In constructing a 'working agreement' with Gladys Beaumont to help her through her crisis, we hope that you will have drawn on her informal network and agreed tasks to enable her to recapture and strengthen that network, since it is an aspect of her life which she recognised was important to her and one which she had neglected. Your agreement may have involved her talking to her neighbour, Janice, and establishing the common ground between them, resolving the difference over the disputed hedge and considering the type of mutual activities they may enjoy when Gladys leaves hospital. It is likely that you will have set Gladys the task of talking more openly with her niece about her life and aspirations and rekindle areas of mutual interest. Similarly you may have encouraged Gladys to agree to talk more freely to the members from her local church who are visiting her, in order to reopen opportunities in her community which to her regret she has shunned of recent. This leads us to a discussion on networking and networking skills.

Networking skills

Networking skills in social work have increased in importance, particularly at the formal level between agencies, as the government in its modernising agenda (DoH, 1998) promotes the 'joined up thinking' between linked organisations, such as those in health and social care. Effective networking from an Adult Social Services perspective is not new. Professional networking and liaison between agencies draws on conventional social work interpersonal and communication skills. This does not stop at practitioner level; Coulshed's (1990) work on management in social services indicated that female managers are particularly skilled in this area.

The emphasis in this section, however, is on the skills on which social workers draw in harnessing, supporting and understanding the informal network such as the one we refer to above in the case of Gladys Beaumont. Approaching service users as, first and foremost, people at the centre of their own informal networks, in terms of family, friends and neighbours, and finding ways to harness these community resources was a key aspect of the Barclay Report (1982); a seminal report in terms of the development of key aspects of professional social work. The role of the informal support systems and its contribution to care in the community was recognised in the White Paper *Caring for People* (DoH, 1989) as the following quotation indicates: *The Government acknowledges that the great bulk of community care is provided by friends, family and neighbours* (para 1.9). Guidance to practitioners (SSI, DoH, 1991a) emphasised the importance of the social network and support systems, and stressed that as part of the comprehensive assessment, service users' needs were to be understood *in their social context, which extends beyond the contribution of direct carers to a wider set of social relations* (page 59). Building onto and harnessing the strengths and resource of the informal network continues to be an important social work skill (Coulshed and Orme, 2006) and one which Smale and Tuson (1993) developed. They stressed the importance of working in partnership with people and service users in local communities (page 40) and put forward models for care managers to work effectively from this baseline. Their 'exchange model' starts with the premise that people are *expert in their own problems* and will know more about themselves, their resources and networks than would the practitioner. The latter will bring expertise in terms of knowledge of the welfare systems, and have skills in problem-solving and developing packages of care. The key problem-solving skill of the practitioner/care manager within this model is to work with the informal and formal networks which surround and engage with the service user, and work out a compromise community care based solution which draws on strengths and interests of all the key participants. This process is described as follows:

> *This involves negotiating with a range of people – from the dependent person, their immediate carers and other people in the community, to service providers from different agencies and professions. Instead of the worker making 'an assessment' and organising care and support for people, which carries the implicit assumption of control,* the worker **negotiates to get agreement about who should do what for whom**.
> Smale and Tuson, 1993, (authors' emphasis)

McDonald (2006) sees theoretical links between community networking skills and those of radical social work, since they both have the capacity to emphasise the importance of collective action and draw out the perception that individual problems are linked to political issues. Payne (2005, page 155) makes the theoretical links between networks and networking and systems theories. Citing Walton's work (1986), he emphasises the importance of *analysing networking within social support systems* both at the formal and informal level, in order to monitor and help those members of the local community who are in need.

Networking skills continue to be an important element of care management since the social and care networks of the service user are an important aspect of the assessment. Developing networking skills can require great sensitivity and insight. Some practitioners find that drawing family trees and friendship diagrams and networks with service users helps to create a useful road map. However, assessing a person's informal friendship or kinship network may not be a straightforward matter. Regularity of contact may say little about the quality and elasticity of the relationship. Payne (1995) reflects that *very close relationships may involve only occasional contacts, and supportive people may live at considerable distance but offer emotional security because they exist and are prepared to help out* (page 101). In a similar vein he comments that assessors of networks must be careful not to make assumptions about the transferability of relationships from one setting to another, for example relationships based on friendship and social activities may not transfer into those based on caring (Payne, 1995, page 113).

ACTIVITY **4.3**

First, thinking about your own networks, construct an ecomap (see Chapter 2) which reflects the friends, relatives and acquaintances in your network. Indicate the ways in which these relationships are important to you and how often you are likely to be in contact on a monthly basis.

Secondly, if you were involved in a serious road traffic accident, whose support would you draw on from your network and why?

The learning point here is that people with whom you spend social time may not be the ones you would wish to have 'a hands on care' relationship with you, and perhaps neither would they be willing or able.

A linked point is that this personal knowledge of your own network is likely to affect how you approach engaging with the informal network of service users when developing care plans (see Chapter 3).

Advocacy

The same premise which we applied to understanding informal networking applies to the concept of advocacy, that is, to quote Smale and Tuson (1993, page 13) *people are, and always will be the expert on themselves*. Within a social work context, it is the service users who should define their own needs and dictate wherever possible how their needs should be met. Early practice guidance (SSI, DoH, 1991a) was intent on promoting service user participation in the assessment process but recognised that not all service users are in the same position:

> *Some users will have a clear understanding of their needs; others will have a more ill-defined view of them or the cause of their difficulties; yet others will require the support of representatives to express their feelings.*
> (SSI, DoH, 1991, para 3.30, page 50)

The guidance goes on to explain the types of service users who are not able to express their views, and who may benefit from independent representation, such as people from minority ethnic groups, people with severe learning disabilities, or who have dementia (para 3.27, page 51). The vehicle for achieving this is the introduction of advocacy schemes to ensure that care managers work closely with independent representatives. The guidance noted that:

> *This will mean ensuring that representatives have access to the necessary information, are able to consult appropriate persons to establish the best interests of the individual and have a safe-guarded role in contributing to the decision-making process.*
> (para 3.28, page 52)

Interpreting this role into the care management process, it would seem that this is not the right role for the care manager given the extensive agency and professional brief which they have to fulfil. Indeed, Payne (1995) argues that care managers may think that they act in the best interests of the service user, but their roles are proscribed and they are unlikely to be in the best position to promote the preferred wishes of the service user (page 193). He states unequivocally that advocates and advocacy groups need to be completely separate from the agency providing the service in order to be able to take an independent stance (page 193).

In terms of theory, strategies that promote advocacy which are also linked to concepts of user empowerment, draw on theories of radical social work and anti-discriminatory practice. The focus is on power sharing with the service user. Payne (2005) refers to the use of advocacy as part of the movement to discharge people from long-stay hospitals and as an integral part of welfare rights initiatives. See his chapter (14) on Empowerment and Advocacy, pages 295–315, for a fuller exposition of these ideas.

The position of an advocate in social work is of increasing importance. Skills in advocacy are referred to in key role three of the National Occupational Standards. This important facet of the social work perspective is not one without tension. As Payne (1995, page 192) states *The essential difference between advocacy and, say, negotiating on a client's behalf is that advocacy occurs in a situation in which there is opposition*.

Although advocacy has been an important part of the social work process for considerable time, it remains ill-defined and there is little evaluation of the procedure (Brandon and Brandon, 2001). Earlier evaluation (Harding and Beresford, 1996) indicated that service users and carers value the process and the service. We draw on Brandon and Brandon's stages of advocacy to help give you a steer on the process.

Stages of advocacy

- explain the advocacy process;

- listen to the client's situation;

- explain the relevant systems – complaints procedures, appeals machinery, outline relevant legislation;

- take instructions;

- seek additional information;

- feed back to the client, exploring together the perceived consequences of possible decisions;

- take revised instructions;

- with permission negotiate with influential person;

- further feed back to client and together explore the consequences;

- prepare for any possible litigation e.g. ombudsman;

- evaluate the whole process to learn necessary lessons.
(Stages taken from Brandon and Brandon, 2001, page 68).

Brandon and Brandon (2001) emphasise the fact that it may not be necessary to follow all the stages indicated. The sequels and the outcome of the process will depend on the degree of difficulty of the case. So, for example, an advocate acting on behalf of Gladys Beaumont at the review stage of a care plan (see Chapter 5) is unlikely to take the case as far as the ombudsman. Brandon and Brandon reinforce the point that in order to empower the service user the skilled advocate needs to draw on expert communication skills, particularly those of listening accurately to the service user's perspective and needs. It is then not a question of putting these needs and wants through a professional filter, neither is it the role of the advocate at the outset to broker compromise solutions. Rather they are required to pay close attention to the expressed wish as the following quotation illustrates:

> *The advocate should **take instructions** (authors' emphasis). This sounds reasonably simple but it isn't. He or she is being 'instructed' by the client to undertake certain agreed actions. That means that there has been an exploration and explanation by the advocate and professional in which the client is perceived as the 'dominant' partner. It is their grievance and their life.*
> (Brandon and Brandon, 2001, page 71)

At every turn the advocate needs to feed back to the service user the results of their enquiries, involving and including them in person wherever possible. If initial instructions have to be modified, negotiations entered into and compromises reached, it is at the behest of the service user. Brandon and Brandon stress the importance of carefully evaluating and learning from the end result from a user perspective and that these processes should be linked to annual independent reviewing procedures (page 74).

The personal assistant (normally referred to as a P.A.) within a system of Direct payments (DP) is likely to be in a strong position to take on aspects of the advocacy role, should those services be required by the service user. The latter is normally responsible for setting up the working agreement and would decide on this aspect of the contract. There is more discussion on DP in chapter five.

C H A P T E R   S U M M A R Y

In this chapter you have been introduced to a range of interventions that can be used effectively in social work. We have illustrated these by way of our two developing case studies. Before continuing the book to consider the importance of reviewing and evaluating what you have done as a social worker, it would be useful to spend a few minutes reflecting on the ways in which task-centred practice, cognitive behavioural work, crisis intervention, networking and advocacy approaches can be adapted to other situations and service use groups.

Adams, R (2003) Social work and empowerment. 3rd edition. Basingstoke: Palgrave.

This is an overview of the concept of empowerment and its importance to social work practice.

Marsh, P and Doel, M (2005) The Task-Centred Book. London: Routledge.

This is a very practical and accessible book that puts centre stage the voice of people who use and those who deliver services.

O'Hagan, K (1986) Crisis intervention in social services. Basingstoke: Macmillan.

Whilst this book may seem a little dated, it offers a thorough view of crisis intervention, its history, development and theory, and grounds this in social work practice in the UK.

Payne, M (2005) Modern Social Work Theory. 3rd edition. Basingstoke: Palgrave Macmillan.

The definitive book to describe, explain and critique social work theory in a comprehensive way. It is a book that will benefit students throughout their studies.

Sheldon, B (1995) Cognitive-behavioural therapy. London: Routledge.

This is not an easy book for students at the beginning of a social work programme but it is worth persevering with. Sheldon covers all aspects of behavioural and cognitive behavioural work from assessment, planning, intervention and review.

Chapter 5
Reviews and the evaluation of practice

Introduction

In this chapter the importance of the review meeting and case review will be examined. What is the role of the social worker in a review and how does it link with the processes of assessment, planning and intervention? Under what circumstances are reviews undertaken and who should or could be involved? This chapter will look at the ways in which social workers can assist service users to give their views to reviews and will consider the importance of communication skills and rights of service users and carers.

You will explore ways of reviewing and evaluating social work practice and be asked to consider the potential effects of working with other professions and with informal carers and service users in carrying out reviews and evaluations of work undertaken. Student social workers, and experienced practitioners, often have many anxieties about reviewing and evaluating their work in a systematic way. In an effective review and evaluation of work undertaken, practice is subject to scrutiny and outcomes and objectives are measured. Whilst this can be a somewhat daunting process, it emphasises accountability and allows practitioners to develop knowledge and skills in determining what works in which circumstances. In these days of increased accountability and audit it is essential that social workers evaluate their practice. This can have the added bonus of ensuring that practice is amended to achieve agreed goals and that social work is promoted as effective to other professions and the wider public.

In this chapter you will be invited to consider how to evaluate an intervention plan in child and family work and social work with adults. Current guidance, research and advice on effective review will be provided and activities will help you to make links between knowledge and practice throughout this chapter. A particular focus will concern the recording of assessments, plans and interventions and how effective, clear recording can assist in review and evaluation of work done. The importance of simple recording schedules and accessibility of written style will be considered. Service user involvement in the intervention process will be emphasised through student centred activities.

You will be asked to question the purpose and use of review and evaluation, especially in respect of care and control issues, bureaucracy and management. You will also be encouraged to consider ways in which they might develop processes for evaluating your own practice and development as beginning professionals.

In the first part of the chapter you will consider why we need to evaluate and review the practice of social work. You will look at some of the external and internal pressures for evaluation, and matters relating to 'effectiveness'. This will be followed by an examination of a number of evaluative strategies and methods for use within social work practice and how you might begin to use them.

Why evaluate social work practice?

Social work is complex and diverse, and the roles and tasks allotted to it are equally varied. This has been recognised for some time as fundamental to qualifying education as shown in the following statement by the previous professional body for social work (Central Council for Education and Training in Social Work (CCETSW):

The purpose of social work is to enable children, adults, families, groups and communities to function, participate and develop in society. Social workers practise in a society of complexity, change and diversity, and the majority of people to whom they provide services are amongst the most vulnerable and disadvantaged in that society. Social workers are employed by a range of statutory, voluntary and private organisations, and work in collaboration with colleagues from allied professions and departments, as part of a network of welfare, health, housing, education and criminal justice provision.
(CCETSW, 1995, page 2)

The tasks and responsibilities that social workers carry range from assessment, planning, to intervention and the provision of services. Social workers work with children and families, the supervision of offenders within the community, adults with physical disabilities, learning disabilities and mental health problems to older people within the community and within institutional care. There are also a range of ways in which social workers attempt to make a difference as indicated in the British Association of Social Workers' *Code of ethics* (2002):

> *(Social workers) work with, on behalf of, or in the interests of people to enable them to deal with personal and social difficulties and obtain essential resources and services. Their work may include, but is not limited to, interpersonal practice, groupwork, community work, social development, social action, policy development, research, social work education and supervisory and managerial functions in these fields.*
> (BASW, 2002, pages 1–2)

The very range of social work practice demands that some understanding of the relative effectiveness of each task is undertaken. The importance of working effectively to protect vulnerable people is stressed in the new degree:

> *Social workers deal with some of the most vulnerable people in our society at times of greatest stress. There can be tragic consequences if things go wrong. Social workers often get a bad press. What they do not get is day to day coverage of the work they do to protect and provide for some of the most vulnerable people in our society.*
> (Department of Health, 2002a, page i)

It is important, therefore, that social workers are educated in ways of reviewing their work and reflecting on outcomes so that practice can be continually improved.

ACTIVITY 5.1

Think of some of the reasons why social work should be evaluated and reviewed. Compile a list of some of these and prioritise the reasons. Undertaking this activity may also give you insight into some of the ways you understand social work.

You may have stressed the accountability side or the necessity of providing cost-effective services. You may have included on your list ethical reasons. There are many reasons why social work practice is evaluated and many justifications for it. To a large extent, these are determined by the agency you are working in, your own personal value base and your knowledge. There are some concerns that research and evaluation has not been highlighted sufficiently in the post-qualifying education framework for social work and an increasing worry that research and evaluation skills, necessary to developing and enhancing the services provided by social workers, are being neglected. The following discussion will provide a number of reasons why social work should be evaluated.

Cheetham et al. (1992) describe two pressures that impinge upon social workers to evaluate the effectiveness of their work. These comprise external pressures and internal pressures. These pressures exert an influence on all aspects of social work.

External pressures

There is a continuing demand for resources to be better targeted and value for money to be achieved. Often, public bodies scrutinise the ends, means and costs of these services within the public welfare sector. The *Best Value* initiative arising from Part I of the Local Government Act 1999 has promoted economy and efficiency within social work practice and health care. There is also an increasing demand for information about the effectiveness of services and also the possibility and implications of different choices of service provision. There has been a growth in the voice of the consumer, and a corresponding concern for economic efficiency and accountability where public spending is an issue. It is unfortunate, as Cheetham et al. (1992) point out, that the more positive accounts of social work practice appear to have been ignored whilst many studies emphasise the difficulties and problems arising from practice. This is still the case fifteen years on!

Internal pressures for evaluation

External pressures may be seen by some as representing a greater degree of managerial control over social work and social care. For some it may be a way of defending social work against attack and ensuring social work's continued existence. Internal pressures for evaluation, however, arise from a general ethical and professional obligation on social workers to do their best for service users and carers and to offer the kind of help and support that is most likely to be effective in each particular case.

Such considerations are also included in the *Code of ethics for social work* produced by the British Association of Social Workers (BASW) (2002). Social workers should *maintain and expand their competence in order to provide quality service and accountable practice* (3.5.2b) and *aim for the best possible standards of service provision and be accountable for their practice* (4.3b). These principles cover the need for social workers to justify work according to agency policy and procedure and also to provide effective intervention to service users.

The GSCC *Code of practice for social care workers* (2002) adds to the need for skills in reviewing, evaluating and improving practice. An approach that builds on prior experience and reflection will help to protect and promote the rights of service users and carers, develop a greater degree of public trust in social work and is instrumental in social workers being accountable for the quality of their work and take responsibility for maintaining and improving their knowledge and skills (GSCC, 2002, page 6).

Effectiveness

The concept of effectiveness warrants some exploration. Different ideas about effectiveness derive from particular ways of thinking about the way the world operates. Different people with different roles in the social care system have different expectations, roles and responsibilities. Therefore, different people have different interpretations of what effectiveness might mean for them. What is success for one may not be so for another. Users of social services may want to know what they are getting out of the work being done. A manager of a social services team may want to know how their money is being spent and whether it is meeting agency and policy guidelines. An individual social worker might be concerned to give a young person the skills and capacity to make choices, whilst a local neighbourhood might want to be assured of protection from that same young person!

↓ quote

A useful working definition of effectiveness is that social work is effective in so far as it achieves its intended aims and objectives. Using such a definition would link with good assessment and planning to ensure that the social work agreed and completed achieved the outcomes that were set. Understanding effectiveness in this way may, however, leave out consideration of the impact of social policies on the lives of service users and carers and to evaluate social work in a more general sense must involve the broader context of social policy.

ACTIVITY 5.2

Write down what you think effectiveness means in relation to social work practice and intervention. Think of possible ways you might review this.

Comment

The activity above may draw a number of different responses. If you have some experience of working in a health or social care environment, you may have related your thoughts back to reviews and indicators set by your agency. You may on the other hand consider effectiveness to relate to user satisfaction rather than agency outcomes. It is likely that whatever you thought of has some relevance to our understanding of effective and how it might be reviewed. The important point to note is that how we measure effectiveness and how we review our work depends on the position we start from and there are other valid approaches to be taken into account.

Reviewing work in children and families social work

In child care, review and evaluation is noted as central to good practice. Reviews may take place when a child or young person is looked after by the local authority. These reviews are statutory and form part of the expected work of social workers in planning and revising plans for children and young people. There are child protection reviews to determine the level of support and protection a child, young person and family need. When events go wrong there is a system of serious case review to determine what lessons can be learned and how practice can be changed in the future. We will explore these different types of review below and illustrate how you might begin to review your casework by references to the developing case study of Melissa and Rebecca. It is also important that social workers review their practice with individual cases and evaluate what they are doing and how effective their practice is in achieving agreed goals. We have seen this in respect of task-centred work and behavioural work with Rebecca and Melissa and will review the evaluation of casework towards the end of this section.

Reviews in child care

Reviews are wider than individual cases. For instance, the duty of a local authority to review day care and related services in consultation with health, voluntary agencies and other interested parties is clearly stated in the guidance accompanying the Children Act 1989 (Department of Health, 1991a). In the process for joint planning and commissioning, monitoring and reviewing the outcomes of services is set in the context of annual per-formance assessments, Joint Area Reviews and also self-monitoring which is intended to develop an improvement culture within services. However, it is usually individual cases that we consider when thinking about reviews.

Statutory child care reviews

Local authorities are empowered by the Review of Children's Cases Regulations 1991 to make provision for reviews of child care cases where the child is looked after by the local authority. The guidance relating to family placements gives a clear definition of reviews which illustrates their importance as a key element of social work practice.

> *Reviews form part of a continuous planning process – reviewing decisions to date and planning future work. The purpose of the review is to ensure that the child's welfare is safeguarded and promoted in the most effective way throughout the period he is looked after or accommodated. Progress in safeguarding and providing for the child's welfare should be examined and monitored at every review and the plan for the child amended as necessary to reflect any significant change.*
> (Department of Health, 1991b, 8.1, page 80)

Review is seen, therefore, as a continuous process that considers what has been achieved from the planning stage and revises or refines plans accordingly, similar to an action-plan-ning or action-research cycle. This requires the social worker to develop a number of skills:

- planning;

- negotiation and consultation;

- information gathering;

- discussion and analysis;

- replanning.

The guidance offers an outline of the process that should be followed including a broad agenda for the review meeting which should deal with three core elements: the progress made in achieving the plan, any need for change and the possible reallocation of tasks or change in the child or young person's status. The last item for consideration relates to the possibility of discharging any order existing in respect of the child or young person (see Johns, 2007, for a greater explanation of the law relating to children). The guidance is clear that children and parents should be as fully involved as possible in the decision-making process, that plans should be structured and that the process should itself be subject to a system of checks. Good practice is promoted in accounting for communica-tion and language difficulties and ensuring that written information and an agenda are sent to all participants prior to the review meeting and that records are kept. The review is there to make plans that continue to safeguard the child.

The timing and minimum frequency of reviews are specified. A first review must be held four weeks after a child or young person begins to be looked after by the local authority and again three months after this. Following the second review, reviews should be carried out at least every six months. This is designed to ensure the process is continuous and that changes in the child or young person's circumstances are taken into account.

Child protection reviews

The child protection conference represents the key forum in which professionals and families discuss concerns, analyse risks and make recommendations to safeguard children and young people. They happen after a child or young person has been the subject of an investigation under section 47 of the Children Act 1989. Any child protection plan needs to be regularly reviewed if it is to remain effective in promoting the welfare of the child and protect them. Recently, the Department of Health (1999) updated their original document *Working together* (1991c) and specified that child protection reviews should be called three months after the first conference and every six months thereafter. This is intended to keep up the momentum and focus on protecting the child or young person and ensuring that needs are met.

> *The purpose of the child protection review is to review the safety of the child against intended outcomes set out in the child protection plan; to ensure that the child continues adequately to be safeguarded; and to consider whether the child protection plan should continue in place or should be changed.*
> (Department of Health, 1999, 8.2, page 87)

The review can decide to take a child or young person off the register and then makes recommendations for their continued protection. The importance of the child protection review is that it is a multidisciplinary meeting involving all those who have interest in the well-being of the child or young person including the parents and children where possible.

Case reviews

These are also known as *Part 8* or *serious case reviews*. These are called whenever an incident that led to the death of a child occurred, where abuse is suspected or confirmed or when there is a child protection issue that is likely to be of major public concern. In these circumstances a review is carried out individually by each agency involved and the Area Child Protection Committee then produces an overall review.

Case reviews are designed to:

- establish whether there are lessons to be learned from the case about the way in which local professionals and agencies work together to safeguard children;

- identify clearly what those lessons are, how they will be acted upon, and what is expected to change as a result and as a consequence;

- to improve inter-agency working and better safeguard children.
  (Department of Health, 1999, 8.2, page 87)

The review called in respect of Rebecca was not a statutory child care review, she was not 'looked after' by the local authority, nor was it a child protection review or serious case review. However, the importance of the review process should not be lessened as a result. The Climbié Report identified the continued monitoring of performance as being central to good practice.

> *Monitoring performance plays a vital role in delivering good outcomes for children and their families. Robust systems that monitor what is actually taking place and its effectiveness is critical.*
> (Laming, 2003, 17.64, page 357)

The report goes on to take issue with past performance monitoring that concentrates on measurable inputs and quantity related outcomes rather than the quality of social work practice. There was also a suggestion that monitoring processes should be undertaken across services working to protect children.

Monitoring, review and evaluation of social work with children and families have often been marginalised. Children and families, once receiving a service, may drift along without consideration of change. This may happen because of the pressures on staff in other areas, or indeed may result from not wanting to change and adapt if things are seen to be working adequately for fear of being blamed if things go wrong. However, we know that children grow and develop, that families adapt and respond to new situations and if we are to respond appropriately to meet the needs of children and families we must review and evaluate our practice. The Looking after Children forms have been helpful in promoting a continuous process of review and replanning in respect of children looked after by local authorities (Ward, 1995; Bailey, Thoburn and Wakeham, 2002). The seven dimensions of well-being have been integrated into the *Framework for assessment* (Department of Health, Department for Education and Employment, Home Office, 2000), and gradually the process of an integrated review system is being rolled out to all children receiving a statutory service. Using such a process of review is good practice even when there is no statutory involvement. Let us return to the case of Rebecca and Melissa and see how the review process worked for them.

CASE STUDY

In the original plan for Rebecca set out in Chapter 3, it was noted that a review of the social work plan and what had been achieved would take place after the four sessions between Irene and Melissa had taken place. The purpose of this review was to consider what had taken place and to decide whether anything more needed to be done or the plan revised. Throughout the task-centred work, Mandy and Melissa regularly reviewed each session and tasks completed between sessions. This was also reviewed after four weeks to check how she was managing at the young mums' group. However, the casework review undertaken after the four sessions between Irene and Melissa concerned all three aims agreed in the initial plan:

* *Is Irene looking after Rebecca twice a week as agreed to give Rebecca a break?*

* *Has Melissa joined the support group?*

* *How has the work to improve Irene and Melissa's relationship progressed?*

Mandy began to prepare for this review at the outset of her involvement with Melissa and Rebecca by introducing the structured approach to the work they would undertake and by stating clearly that a review would take place within the plan. However, preparations for the review began in earnest during the final two weeks prior to the review. Mandy telephoned June, the health visitor, the child support worker who looked after Rebecca at the family support centre, and Irene and spoke directly with Melissa to arrange a convenient date and time for the review. It was not possible to speak with Rebecca because of her age but her daily routines and patterns were taken into account so that she would not be disrupted by the review. It is important to be sensitive to the needs of all people involved and not to assume that because a person cannot voice their opinions they are not affected by decisions taken.

After having agreed a date and time, Mandy began to collect information for the review. She returned to the assessment and care plan for Rebecca and asked each person involved for their views about the work that had been undertaken. She explained that she would be writing a short report about the work to discuss further at the review and agreed to send it to each person with a formal invitation confirming date and time. She also said that any disagreements with the report or work could be taken up at the review or noted prior to it. To ensure that she reflected the views of those involved as best as possible, however, she summarised her understanding of what they had said after gathering their views.

Mandy asked her team leader, Geoff, to act as chairperson for the review. It is important to have a chair who is slightly removed form the day-to-day aspects of the case. This helps in keeping a focus and ensuring that issues not seen by those directly involved can be picked up. It must be remembered also that review meetings are daunting affairs – for some professionals as well as service users and carers – and the more formal the meeting the greater the potential anxiety. It is the social worker co-ordinating the review and the chair who are responsible for creating a relaxed and welcoming atmosphere so as to encourage service users and carers in putting their points of view forward. Sometimes it is appropriate for a friend or other supportive person to be allowed to accompany service users and carers. Both Melissa and Irene were comfortable with the process, however, having met Geoff before and by his welcome and clear explanation of the review meeting, what it was there to achieve and how it would be run.

Geoff welcomed everyone to the meeting, stating that they were there to review the care plan made in respect of Rebecca. He then asked everyone to introduce themselves and say a little about the ways in which they were involved with Rebecca. Those present were called on to give their views about the plan, and how it had worked. This began with Mandy being asked to speak about her report and was followed by opportunities for the others to add, clarify or question the report. Geoff summarised what was said at frequent intervals to check understanding and to keep the meeting focused. He made sure that everyone was given an opportunity to contribute and when the three points had been covered, and the views of what had been achieved had been made, he moved the review to consider what should be done next.

Irene had begun to offer Melissa one afternoon and one evening breaks from Rebecca each week. Irene was enjoying the contact with her granddaughter and Melissa said that she was able to get time out with friends and felt she had 'a breathing space'. Both of them agreed that this was helped by the open discussions they had together at the family support team and that airing views frankly had helped them see each other's perspective. The family support worker who looked after Rebecca during these sessions reported that Rebecca was a happy and inquisitive baby who seemed to enjoy the company of Irene and Melissa. The health visitor agreed and said that she believed Melissa had been helped by the support she had received from the other mothers at the support group. Melissa agreed and said she did not want to lose that support.

The plans were agreed by the review meeting as having positive results. There did not seem to be a need for any further family sessions or indeed for further social work involvement. However, it was suggested that a revised agreement be made that Irene continues to offer a break to Melissa and that Melissa is able to continue to attend the young mums' group.

ACTIVITY 5.3

Imagine that you are the social worker involved with Rebecca and Melissa. After the review you have been asked to write a letter explaining what the outcomes and agreements made were. Have a go at writing this letter and think of the importance of how issues are worded and phrased.

Comment

Rather than providing you with an example letter to check against for the activity above, it is more important for you to examine what you have written as though you were the person receiving the letter. Is the letter clearly written? Do you set out the reasons why the letter is being written, what it relates to and do you carefully spell out the outcomes that were agreed? Can any of the letter be understood in a different way to the one you intended? If so, re-write that part of the letter until you are sure it will say exactly what you want it to say.

Remember also to check that it is simply written, that jargon is avoided and that sentences are short and to the point. It is possible to write a clear and simple letter conveying all the information you want to get across without being patronising!

Case review and monitoring in adult services

We will now turn to consider how case review and monitoring are used in care management and link this to our developing case study of Gladys Beaumont. In adult services the importance of case monitoring and reviewing cannot be too strongly emphasised. These were the areas that had been neglected prior to the 1990 NHS and Community Care Act (Social Services Inspectorate and Department of Health 1991a, 1991b). As discussed in Chapter 1, prior to the Act, community care services were not seen to be provided in an effective way. A key aspect of this critique was that provision was not tailored to need, since it was not systematically monitored and reviewed. What happened in real terms was that services were arranged and rarely altered unless there was a major incident. As Payne (1995, page 213) comments, *...crises were often reached unnecessarily. The lack of periodic review in many adults' cases meant that they drifted with very little strategic thought about 'what next?'*

Monitoring and reviewing are the fourth and fifth stages in the care management process. They are often linked since the one informs the other. Hence a brief reflection here on the process of monitoring. In 1991 the importance of monitoring was recognised; prior to this time it had been viewed as a passive activity. Following the introduction of care management the function of monitoring was to promote the objectives of the care plan and provide evidence on which the refinement and review of the plan could be based. Signs of difficulties were to trigger early reviews. Close monitoring of this kind coupled with systematic recording was also to provide managers with the framework in which manager/practitioner accountability could be scrutinised (Social Services Inspectorate and Department of Health, 1991a, pages 78–80). This links to the points made about local authority governance and 'top down' bureaucracies discussed in Chapter 3. Checking standards and maintaining high levels of practice were also seen as mechanisms for supporting and enhancing the quality of service for service users and their carers, within systems of long-term care.

In terms of the reviewing stage, the focus of this chapter, early guidance within the care management system (Social Services Inspectorate and Department of Health, 1991a, pages 83–88) had emphasised its importance and had been prescriptive of the process. Reviewing was seen as *the mechanism by which changing needs are identified and services adapted accordingly* (page 83). The process was to be *needs based* taking account of the preferences and needs of the service user and carer. Thus, the form and content of the review were to reflect user sensitivity and needs. Users and carers were to be kept informed of the purpose of the review and to be given the choice to have a representative present. The venue was to be chosen with their needs in mind. Whilst those involved in the original care plan needed to be consulted and to convey their views as appropriate to the review, they need not be present. A large-scale review with its tendency to overpower and be dominated by professionals was not envisaged, unless the situation had reached crisis point and new and complex arrangements were required. Ideally there was to be an independent chair, particularly if there were contentious and conflicting areas. Finally, practitioners were to inform service users and their carers of their rights to complain. In essence the guidance was to promote and empower the view of the service user and carer and keep them at the centre of the process. A schedule and purpose of the review is as follows.

A standard schedule for the recording of reviews

A review record will include the following.

- A review of the achievements of the care plan objectives – by assessing the realism of the original plan and its continuing relevance by checking it against the perceptions of the user and carer and those of the service providers.

- Learn from and examine the reasons for success or failure of the plan.

- Question whether current services have been both cost effective and of the right quality.

- Reassess current needs of the service user and carer.

- Consider whether the eligibility level remains the same – extend, reduce or withdraw services as appropriate and provide full explanation to service user and/or their representative.

- Re-evaluate and revise as appropriate original care plan objectives – setting new short-term objectives for each service provider, bearing in mind the wishes of the user and carer.

- Re-define and renegotiate the service contracts as necessary.

- Re-calculate the cost and revise the budget, subject to management approval, for the period leading to the next review.

- Identify areas where quality of service is deficient.

- Set date for next review.

- Record and share copy of review report with the user and, subject to confidentiality constraints, other contributors to the review.

(Adapted from Social Services Inspectorate and Department of Health 1991a, pages 85–86, paras 7.14–7.23)

Reading through the schedule above you may have reflected on the complexity of the process and of the task. Much preparation and consultation is required before the review. The person responsible for chairing the review will need to draw on competent chairing skills, and also helping and negotiating skills if they are to keep the perspective of the service user central to the process. It should not be a mechanistic task but a real opportunity for participants to reflect, take stock, stand back from what has happened since the assessment, and make changes and adjustments to stated objectives. As Payne (1995) reflects:

> *The longer-term review stage of care management requires a different approach to that of monitoring. Here, the view should be strategic. What has been achieved for the client? What is the right direction now? How have views and attitudes among those involved changed? What are their wishes, especially those of clients and carers, now?*
> (Payne, 1995, page 215)

Facilitating open discussion and harnessing and making sense of new ideas and insights is a creative process. The person responsible for the review will also need to be able to revisit and revise budgets and service specifications and draw on administrative skills which enable them to write a sensitive and yet thorough review report.

Guidance from the Department of Health concerning the review process within the SAP (Department of Health, 2002b, pages 26–27) builds onto the review process described. Within the new arrangements, increased recognition is given to the time frame and the agencies that are likely to be directly involved. For example the new guidance confirms that a review should take place within three months from when social care, health and housing provision were implemented, or alternatively from when major changes to a care plan took place. After this point reviews are to be held at least annually or more frequently if necessary if circumstances dictate. The reference to treatment in two out of the five stated purposes of the revised review reflects the importance of the health agenda. The reference to direct payments also flags up the importance of this development in adult services (Leece, 2000). The redefined purposes of the review are:

- establish how far the support and treatment have achieved the outcomes, set out on the care plan;

- reassess the needs and issues of individual service users;

- help determine users' continued eligibility for support and treatment;

- confirm or amend the current care plan, or lead to closure;

- comment on how individuals are managing direct payments, where appropriate.

The results are to be recorded by agencies drawing on the stated purpose of the review. The care plan will be updated in the light of the review, if the service user remains eligible for ongoing services. Alternatively, reasons for the closure of the case are to be recorded and shared wherever possible with the service user. Fuller guidance on these processes is to be found in the document *Fair access to care services* (Department of Health, 2003a).

Monitoring and Reviewing: room for improvement

Monitoring and review are not uncontentious areas. Lymbery (2005 page 181) cites the fact that the Fair Access to Care Services documentation that includes practice guidance (Department of Health 2003b) 'had to include an injunction to improve the quality of review processes that testifies to the fact that these had been neglected'. Similarly, in her chapter on 'Monitoring and Review' McDonald (2006 pages 61–70) draws on research to illustrate the fact that in practice the two tasks are not viewed as distinctive and even though they are integral to the role and task of care management they are seen as of secondary importance to that of the process of assessment. Further, within the reviewing process she notes that the emphasis is on accountable practice rather than good practice, this, she argues, demonstrates the importance of the procedural nature of the task over and above other elements.

ACTIVITY **5.4**

Gladys Beaumont: review of a realistic care plan?

You are preparing for Gladys Beaumont's review. Think back over the care plan which you wrote for her, or the one which we drafted, and consider what is likely to have gone wrong within the first six weeks of her returning home and why.

Keep your notes and refer to them as we examine the process of the review.

CASE STUDY

Preparation for the review meeting and reflections on Direct Payments

Six weeks after the discharge home a review is to take place in Gladys' home, in order to keep the proceedings as informal as possible. John Brown, an independent reviewing officer, is to be the independent chair and he and Matthew plan to convene a meeting that will not be dominated by professionals. The District Nurse Samantha Smith, the neighbour Janice Brown and an Age Concern volunteer, Meryl Higgins acting as Gladys' advocate will attend. Apologies have been received from Anthea Jones, the niece.

It was Matthew who suggested to Gladys that she invite her volunteer from Age Concern to be present. Meryl has recently re-established contact with Gladys and as a trained advocate is gaining a reputation for her skills in this area. Mathew has known that Gladys is not altogether happy with the care plan, but he was not certain of the extent of her concerns. Gladys had never really opened up and talked to him and he knows that she did not want another care manager, since she felt comfortable with Sarah Jacobs the hospital based care manager and did not want to lose this relationship.

On reflection Matthew wonders if he has been too 'risk averse' with Gladys' care and whether, when the 'enabling service' comes to an end, he should suggest that she considers Direct Payments (DP) as an alternative to services provided directly by the local authority. He's recently been on a training course that's encouraged him to think of the benefits of DP for older people. He now knows that service users are eligible to receive DP providing they are willing and able __with assistance__ to cope, and that this should be taken into account when making an assessment. His line manager is also keen that he should raise the profile of DP in his work since its take up is linked to external performance indicators. Matthew normally ignores these type of comments referring to them as too 'managerialist' but he likes the sound of DP. He's read some leaflets in the office that are written from a user perspective that describe its pros and cons and refers to a local support service that would help Gladys manage the paperwork and the responsibilities of being an employer. He thinks that her neighbour Janice would be interested in part-time work and that she would make a good personal assistant (PA) and thus receive payment for her help and whatever extra Gladys needed. In this way Gladys may feel less beholden and exploitative of her. He reflects that if Janice were able to put Gladys to bed then it could work... He thought that the equivalent of Gladys' current support, that of three visits a day from the care workers would be about 21 DP hours per week. Surely that would be enough he muses? He could also help Gladys advertise for a second PA so that she always had a contingency plan in the event of Janice going off sick or on holiday. Definitely a good idea but dividing up the hours may prove difficult. Nonetheless, he argues that on balance DP would enable Gladys to have more choice and control over her life. He resolves to 'sound out' tentatively these ideas with Gladys and Janice before the review.'

On their way to the meeting Matthew shares his ideas on DP and John tells him how he plans to manage the review. First he 'hears out' the service user; secondly he pulls together the professionals' views; and thirdly he makes decisions and alters the care plan as necessary.

Direct Payments

The legislation for direct payments is embodied in the Community Care (Direct Payments) Act 1996. The Act gave local authorities the power (not as strong as a duty and therefore less enforceable) to implement DP. However, it was not until 2000 that the service was extended, through Statutory instrument 2000/11, to people over 65. Policy and practice guidance that actively encouraged take up, was introduced. There has been no let up on the part of government to run with this initiative for older people. It was viewed as a way of enabling them to manage their own care and to some extent their health conditions. Nonetheless take up has not been robust, due in part to the lack of active promotion of the scheme by social workers and their apparent lack of knowledge about it (Glasby and Littlechild 2002). The strategy for developing services to adults in this way was emphasised in the Green Paper *Independence, well-being and choice* (Department of Health 2005) and in the subsequent White Paper *Our health, our care, our say* (2006). DP is described in the latter as the 'payments given to individuals so that they can organise and pay for the social care services they need, rather than using the services offered by their local authority' (page 210). More information and easy to read leaflets on DP, such as the CSIP (Care Services Improvement Partnership) Direct Payments Uptake Project can be found on the following website:

www.dh.gov.uk/PolicyAndGuidance/OrganisationPolicy/FinanceAndPlanning/ DirectPayments/fs/en

Think about and make a list of the pros and cons of DP in Gladys' case. Read the information on the website above and ask yourself:

1. *What are the responsibilities of the local authority towards Gladys if she was on DP?*

2. *What are Gladys' responsibilities likely to be to the person she employs within a DP framework?*

CASE STUDY

The Review

Phase one – Gladys' concerns

After making certain that everyone knew each other John described his approach. He emphasised that his main task was to review the achievements of the care plan and check out what had worked and what had been less successful. He reminded the meeting of the objectives of the care plan which are:

- *to continue to encourage Gladys in her rehabilitation and work towards her becoming more physically independent and mobile;*

- *to actively seek to help Gladys to change her diet and fully stabilise her diabetes;*

- *to encourage Gladys to lead a more creative and positive life in her community;*

- *to assess the extent to which the six-week trial of the pendant alarm has been successful;*

- *to review the care plan in four weeks or sooner if the home care arrangements break down for any reason.*

He also suggested that direct payments be discussed. Gladys said she felt OK talking about what was working well and not working but those present could tell by the look on her face that she was not pleased with how things were. She sighed and said that she was just getting used to Glynis, her personal carer, calling each day as agreed, they got on well and she looked forward to seeing her. Then Glynis went on holiday for a week and never came back. No one came to tell her what had happened and since then there had been a succession of different workers who often arrived late. Some she felt were intrusive, particularly when they just stood watching her whilst she made breakfast. Gladys thought this was a complete waste of time, when they could be washing the windows or doing something useful. And why did they still keep on coming when she said she was having visitors?

Matthew explained that it was often difficult to maintain continuity of cover during school holidays but agreed to take up the matter. Meryl told the meeting that it was not good practice to put the needs of the service providers before those of the service user. No one disagreed and John continued with the review. He explained to Gladys that the personal carers were right to let her do as much as possible for herself, since working towards her independence was the principal objective of the care plan. He said that personal care was the prime concern of his agency and that currently, due to staff shortages, Adult Social Services did not provide a cleaning service. Meryl said that she thought the agency may be acting illegally by not providing this service.

Gladys had begun to talk about how she felt about her progress at home. From a mobility point of view she said that she had made good progress since she can now transfer her weight and has learned to walk short distances on crutches. She felt nonetheless held back by 'not being allowed' to use her crutches in the house unsupervised. She confirmed that she had made some changes to her diet; she knew what she should eat but admitted to not liking 'healthy' food. Her frustration was that she has good intentions to change her life for the better following the shock of the operation, but that she remained house-bound and dependent on the good will of others, mainly Janice her neighbour. The days at home are long and tedious. On balance, having talked to Matthew, Janice and Meryl and having read the leaflet, she thought direct payments was a better way of arranging service for her and that she'd like to give it a go.

Comment

Staff shortages and staff changes in social care provision continue to create problems that can be unsettling for service users and early guidance had warned against the wishes of users and carers being subordinate to those of service providers (Social Services Inspectorate and Department of Health, 1991a, page 9, para 6.). Similar concerns have been reported by the ombudsman in recent years (McDonald, 2006). In a study which looked at how older people defined a quality service (Joseph Rowntree Foundation, 2000) service users rated highly factors such as staff reliability, continuity of care, continuity of staff and the kindness and understanding of care workers. Given the sensitive nature of the work it is important that service users feel comfortable and secure with staff who attend to their very personal care needs.

As Gladys is making progress, she is also becoming frustrated by the inflexible routine. Flexibility to respond to changing needs and requirements was another key finding from the Rowntree study (2000). The capacity amongst health and social care professionals to respond creatively and flexibly as the situation arises sends a message to service users which is both empowering and anti-oppressive. Similarly the reverse effect may be created by the tendency within current structures to wait until the review occurs before adjustments are made.

With reference to Adult Social Services' obligation to provide a cleaning service, McDonald (2006, page 20) informs us that under Schedule 8 of the NHS Act 1977, the local authority has a statutory duty to provide a home help service which is adequate to the needs of the area. She notes nonetheless that an increasing trend among Adult Social Services is to see their priorities as delivering personal care to vulnerable people, with domestic cleaning very much a secondary role, and only for those with high level needs.

Gladys' frustration with the amount of close supervision required in her rehabilitation raises several good practice issues which are not always easy to square. As Meredith (1995) reflects services can sometimes unwittingly undermine independence (page 179). As practitioners we need to consider whether we have a tendency to be over-protective, ageist and discriminatory towards service users of a particular age. Are people such as Gladys Beaumont allowed to take the same level of risk as other adults in society, or do we treat older people as part of a homogenous group and fail to challenge society's stereo-types? On the other hand are there valid health and medical reasons why close supervision is seen as necessary? (See Ray and Phillips' chapter on critical practice with older people in Adams, Dominelli and Payne, 2002.)

CASE STUDY *continued*

The Review

Phase two: the perspective of the professionals
John was feeling pressured to move the review forward. He was intent on reaching a consensus concerning the strengths and the risks associated with Gladys' situation. The district nurse said that whilst significant progress had been made, she had some concerns and she felt that now was not the right time to consider DP. She said that Gladys had fallen several days ago when, against advice, she was practising using her crutches alone at home; not enough progress had been made to stabilise her diabetes; and that whilst Gladys can now transfer her weight, she remained vulnerable particularly using the bathroom unaided. Gladys interrupted. 'What was the problem' she demanded and added that she was an adult, could do what she liked in her own home and also had a pendent alarm if things went wrong. John suggested, a little provocatively, that the key concerns appeared to be the management of Gladys' health and that therefore social services perhaps could pull back on the intensive care package and work out a more flexible system on a weekly basis depending on Gladys' informal arrangements.

Comment

Negotiating the professional territory between health and social services is not new but has gained impetus (Bradley and Manthorpe, 2000). The Health Act 1999 created the framework for pooling joint budgets and delivering joint services between health and social care, these initiatives were consolidated when care trusts were established and integrated working became of greater importance (for further details see Quinney 2006, particularly chapter 4). Effective interprofessional working is at the heart of the government's 'joined up' agenda as reflected in the content of the SAP (Department of Health, 2002b). Whilst colleagues from different disciplines recognise the importance of working together effectively, their training and professional views may lead to different assessments of a case such as that of Gladys Beaumont. For example, social work training is more likely to lead practitioners to take a holistic view of service users and see them in their broader social context, recognising the ethical dilemmas associated with balancing risks against a service user's rights and desires. Health trained professionals are more likely to focus on physical and health constraints in their assessments. Research (Ramon, 2002) suggests that these inter- professional boundaries are not easy to resolve.

The Review

Phase three: the decisions

John felt that it was time to reach a consensus. He recognised that Gladys' state of health remained uncertain in spite of the evident progress, and social and health care services would need to continue to work closely together. He wished to allay the concerns of the district nurse, and her fears that Adult Social Services may be bidding to withdraw its support. He proposed that the review kept Gladys, eligibility at the same level, thus reflecting the needs of the case and the priority given to it at agency level. However he did not dismiss Gladys' wish to move to direct payments. He recognised her rights to have more choice and control over her life and the importance of her continuing to eat more healthy food and improve her level of mobility, which he thought would more likely continue if she felt in control. Gladys said that she was confident that, with help she could work towards setting up DP to her satisfaction. She'd done her homework: Janice had agreed to be her PA and did not think there would be a problem assisting her in and out of bed. Meryl was talking her through the DP paperwork. However, she was the first to agree, much to the relief of the agency workers present, that she would take it a 'step at a time'. Thus in the meantime John moved to put the more flexible service plan into operation as indicated above. He suggested that part of his budget could be vired and used to help fund outside activities and some transport for Gladys. There was talk of a health colleague finding a lighter wheel chair; of an aromatherapy class at one of the resource centres that was well received; of some interesting courses run by the University of the Third Age. At the end of the review John informed Gladys that if she was not satisfied with the way her case was being dealt with then she had the right to complain. He thanked everyone for attending. Finally, he said that the date of the next review would be fixed once it was known when Gladys would move to DP.

Practice Challenges and Reflections on Recent Green and White Papers

We have not dealt with the detail of how this care plan will be bolted down, written up, divided once more between informal carers and professional colleagues or be translated into a DP framework. We leave it unfinished so that you, the reader, can write a range of endings and perhaps fill in the weekly care chart in different more creative ways. We leave you with the reflection that complex cases such as that of Gladys Beaumont, cases which straddle health and social care and which include chronic health conditions, do not lend themselves to short-term resolution. One of the guiding principles which underpins care management is that it was set up to respond to the longer-term needs of vulnerable older people (Challis, Darton, Johnson, Stone and Traske, 1995). As social workers we have to listen more carefully to what people say they want and give them more choice of services, within models of service delivery that harness technology. We also need to think more creatively about how to improve access to and take up of direct payments for adult service users, particularly by those who are older (Department of Health 2005). These are some of the ideas that have been promoted in the government's Green Paper *Independence, well-being and choice* (2005) and White Paper *'Our health, our care, our say: a new direction for community services' (2006)*. These new and revised initiatives are not without challenge to practitioners, not least since it is the government's intention not to provide additional funding for its new vision of social care for adults (Department of Health 2005).

In presenting and building the case stage by stage, we hope we have gone some way to explain the evolving process and particularly reinforced the importance of listening carefully to the service user and keeping her expressed needs and wishes at the heart of the matter.

Casework evaluation

Social workers do not simply operate as bureaucrats following explicitly laid out agency procedures. There is an emphasis in social work on developing professional judgement, critical thinking skills and reflecting on the ways in which social work progresses. There are professional, developmental and ethical reasons for reviewing and evaluating individual casework, as Alston and Bowles (2003) state:

> *Workers in the welfare field must be accountable for the service they provide, the resources they expend and the outcomes they achieve. Accountability is expected by governments, clients and taxpayers. Evaluation and accountability have always been important concepts for social workers. Handled effectively program evaluation gives us the means to develop techniques for ensuring our practice is enhanced and effective and allows us to incorporate accountability and transparency into our practice. Program evaluation techniques allow us to be more effective and efficient workers, which can only enhance our work with clients and the communities we serve.*
> (Alston and Bowles, 2003, page 140)

It is important to gain an understanding of the importance of the ways research can inform practice and you will be encouraged as a social worker to develop *research-mindedness*. This means you will be able to recognise that research is important but also to be able to undertake your own research concerning your practice with the intention of improving and updating it.

It is not possible in this chapter to give a detailed account of practitioner research but it is important to note that attention to ways in which you might evaluate your practice is part of the process of developing good and effective social work practice. By reference to Rebecca and Melissa we will introduce a visual way of considering whether an intervention is making a difference, note the importance of user satisfaction and the importance of reflection and *practice wisdom* or developing an appreciation of the art involved in improving social work practice.

In Chapter 4 you were introduced to a graphic display of targets of your intervention with Melissa and Rebecca the second time they had contact with social workers. The number of times that Rebecca asked Melissa to play when she was having a rest in the evening was noted. This formed a 'baseline' period or a display of how things looked before the intervention.

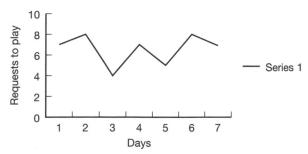

Requests to play

By continuing the monitoring of the situation, recording the number of times Rebecca asked Melissa to play during the intervention period, changes could be clearly shown.

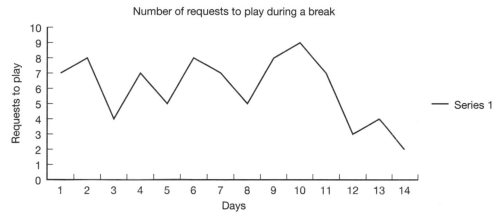

Requests to play over time

Whilst this does not 'prove' that the intervention was successful it provides a visual display of what happened and an indication that change occurred during the intervention period. There are more complex ways of assessing whether or not your intervention was responsible for the change but it is best to start simple. Further and more detailed information can be found in Sheldon (1995).

The advantage of tracking changes like this is that they help in showing to service users that there is a difference in the situation but also it helps you to judge whether or not your practice needs to adapt. However, interventions cannot be judged solely from the perspective of the social worker.

User perspectives

Since the seminal work undertaken by Mayer and Timms (1970) the service user perspective has grown in importance in social work. However, asking service users and carers what they think about services received or how satisfied they are is fraught with difficulties. Partly, this stems from the different ways in which we might understand 'satisfaction' and partly from the likelihood that service users may feel unable to give a true opinion because they do not want to upset the social worker or, indeed, they would like to upset the social worker, or because people may fear having services withdrawn if they express dissatisfaction. Despite these concerns it is important to give service users and carers an opportunity to present their views and encouragement to do so in an honest and open way.

Social workers may also find they are required to undertake studies from the perspective of service users to fulfil the Quality Assurance demands of their teams and employing agencies.

Pluralistic evaluation

Traditional ways of evaluating intervention or social work projects tend to look at the views of only one party involved, perhaps those of the social worker, the service user or the carer. They often do not include the views of other professions. Pluralistic evaluation (Smith and Cantley, 1985) acknowledges that there are many, and sometimes conflicting, opinions and the ways of judging success may differ whether you are a service user, service provider, carer, practitioner or manager. In practical terms, pluralistic evaluation involves collecting the views and opinions of all those involved including the different notions of success. Whilst you may not use such an approach in your casework it is important to be aware of the many different ways an outcome can be assessed.

C H A P T E R   S U M M A R Y

This chapter has covered two areas of social work practice that are often relegated to last place in the minds of many social workers. Whilst this may be understandable in some respects, people have busy case loads and pressure to take on new cases, it is not defendable. The situations in which service users and carers find themselves are ever-changing and need regular review to ensure that services provided are the ones that are most likely to be effective in producing change. Also, it is important that social workers continually strive to improve their practice, and are able to demonstrate to service users, carers and their employers that what they are doing is working. Attention to a regular system of review and monitoring of casework is part of good practice. Developing a research-minded approach to one's practice and development can assist the overall process that we have begun to describe throughout this book.

FURTHER READING

Department of Health (1991a) The Children Act guidance and regulations. Volume 2. Family support, day care and educational provision for young children. London: HMSO.

Department of Health (1991b) The Children Act guidance and regulations. Volume 3. Family placements. London: HMSO.

These two volumes form part of a comprehensive range of guidance issued in respect of the Children Act 1989. They are useful in providing basic information and an understanding of the Children Act in practice.

Department of Health (1999) Working together to safeguard children. A guide to inter-agency working to safeguard and promote the welfare of children. London: TSO.

This volume updated earlier guidance and provides information designed to enhance good practice and prevent communication difficulties that have beleaguered helping professions.

Laming, H (2003) The Victoria Climbié inquiry report. Cm 5730. London: The Stationery Office.

McDonald, A (2006) Understanding Community Care: a guide for social workers. 2nd edition Basingstoke: Macmillan.

This book is a critical overview of community care which is grounded in good practice concerns and guidance.

Conclusion

This book attempts to outline key elements of social work practice in a range of settings. It does not seek to be comprehensive but to prepare you for future and continued study. There is a danger that the parts we have described may be taken apart from the process that makes up social work practice. We have stressed throughout the book that assessment is part of the process of intervention in another person's life and that planning begins before the assessment starts. Plans for the review are made at the outset to the work. What we have attempted to avoid is a piecemeal approach and to see the elements that we have included as linking with each other forming part of a much wider whole: social work practice (see Parker, 2007a).

Of course, in practice you may be asked to concentrate on one aspect of social work as opposed to others, but the process is still there. Whilst we need to see the process of practice integrated with its component parts, similarly we must not lose sight of the bigger picture of social work within which critical and emancipatory practice is placed. It is a central concern and challenge to social welfare and social justice in many modern and developing states and countries.

The building blocks of practice and the developing themes and stages set out in this book are likely to remain central within the new framework of social work education and training. However, whilst the guiding principles underlying these aspects of practice may remain relatively constant, the procedural details and guidelines are likely to be refined in response to the changing needs and perspectives of service users and carers, and the changing professional, cultural and political tides. Such is the speed of change in social work that many of the procedures and much of the guidance provided by government are likely to change several times throughout your education and certainly when working as a qualified social worker. We have made an assumption throughout the book that you will be increasingly aware of this factor and that you are embarking on a future professional role in which learning and professional development are life-long. We hope that as a consequence of reading the book and participating in the activities that we have further encouraged you down this path, and that your development as a beginning practitioner is based on a commitment to this process of exploration. We hope that you will be in a position to be able to, and motivated to want to, access professional and academic journals and websites to help keep you well briefed and current in your thinking and practice, and motivated to continue to refine your thinking and find new ways to link practice to the best theories around. Indeed your future registration requirements demand it! It is our intention that you will be in a postion to transfer learning from this work into your first job as a social worker and inform your induction and beyond. We also would like to think that we have started the process of enabling you to become a critical and effective practitioner: that is, a social worker who is able and willing to 'think out of the box'; one who sees further than the local practice guidance and procedures; one who makes the links between debates in parliament today and social work practice tomorrow and can see the value of engaging in those debates. Social work does not stand still, and neither is it bound by geography and territory. Critical practice when held up to the light should be more than the sum of its parts. It should also reflect the commitment of both social work as a profession and individual social workers, to peaceful co-existence and social justice for all.

References

Adams, R (2003) Social work and empowerment. 3rd edition. Basingstoke: Palgrave.

Adams, R, Dominelli, L and Payne, M (eds) (2002) Social work: themes, issues and critical debates. 2nd edition. Basingstoke: Palgrave.

Aguilera, DC and Messick, JM (1974) Crisis intervention. Theory and methodology. St Louis, Missouri: C.V. Mosby and Co.

Aguilera, DC and Messick, JM (1982) Crisis intervention therapy for psychological emergencies. New York: Plume.

Alston, M and Bowles, W (2003) Research for social workers: an introduction to methods. 2nd edition. London: Routledge.

Audit Commission (2000) Charging with care. London: The Stationery Office.

Bailey, S, Thoburn, J and Wakeham, H (2002) Using the 'looking after children' dimensions to collect aggregate data on well-being. Child and Family Social Work, 7, 3, 189–201.

Baldwin, BA (1979) Crisis intervention: an overview of theory and practice. The Counseling Psychologist, 8, 2, 43–52.

Banks, S (2004) Ethics, Accountability and the Social Professional. Basingstoke: Palgrave MacMillan.

Barclay Report (1982) Social workers: their roles and tasks. London: Bedford Square Press.

Barker, P (1986) Basic Family Therapy. Oxford: Blackwell.

Bartlett, H (1970) The common base of social work practice. New York: National Association of Social Workers.

Bradley, G (1997) Translating research into practice. Social Work and Social Science Review, 7, 1, 3–12.

Bradley, G. (2003) Administrative Justice and Charging for Long-term Care. British Journal of Social Work. 33, 641–657.

Bradley, G. (2005) Movers and Stayers in Care Management in Adult Services. British Journal of Social Work 35, 511–530.

Bradley, G and Manthorpe, J (1997) Dilemmas of financial assessment. Birmingham: Venture Press.

Bradley, G and Manthorpe, J (eds) (2000) Working on the fault line. Birmingham: Venture Press.

Bradley, G, Manthorpe, J, Stanley, N and Alaszewski, A (1996) Training for care management: using research to identify new directions. Issues in Social Work Education, 16, 2, 26–44.

Bradley, G, Penhale, B, Manthorpe, J, Parkin, A, Parry, N and Gore, J (2000) Ethical dilemmas and administrative justice: perceptions of social and legal professionals towards charging for residential and nursing home care. Hull: University of Hull.

Brandon, D and Brandon, T (2001) Advocacy in social work. Birmingham: Venture Press.

Brayne, H and Carr, H (2005) Law for social workers, 9th edition. Oxford: Oxford University Press.

British Association of Social Workers (BASW) (2002) The Code of Ethics for Social Work. Birmingham: BASW.

Brownell, P (1997) The application of the culturagram in cross-cultural practice with elder abuse victims. Journal of Elder Abuse and Neglect, 9, 2, 19–33.

Burnham, J (1986) Family therapy. London: Tavistock.

Caplan, G (1961) An approach to community mental health. New York: Grune and Stratton.

Carkhuff, R (1987) The art of helping. 6th edition. Amerhurst, MA: Human Resource Development Press.

Central Council for Education and Training in Social Work (CCETSW) (1995) DipSW Rules and Requirements for the Diploma in Social Work. CCETSW Paper 30. London: CCETSW.

Challis, D, Darton, R, Johnson, L, Stone, M and Traske, K (1995) Care management and health care of older people. Aldershot: Ashgate.

Cheetham, J, Fuller, R, McIvor, G and Petch, A (1992) Evaluating social work effectiveness. Buckingham: Open University Press.

Cigno, K (2002) Cognitive-behavioural practice. In Adams R, Dominelli L and Payne M (eds) Social work: themes, issues and critical debates. 2nd edition. Basingstoke: Palgrave/Open University Press.

Cigno, K and Bourn, D (eds) (1998) Cognitive behavioural social work in practice. Aldershot: Ashgate/Arena.

Clifford, D (1998) Social assessment theory and practice: a multi-disciplinary framework. Aldershot: Ashgate.

Compton, B and Galaway, B (1975) Social work processes. Homewood, IL: Dorsey Press.

Congress, E (1994) The use of culturagrams to assess and empower culturally diverse families. Families in Society, 75, 9, 531–40.

Cooper, B (2000) The measure of a competent child care social worker? Journal of Social Work Practice, 14, 2, 113–24.

Coulshed, V (1990) Management in social work. London: Macmillan.

Coulshed, V and Orme, J (2006) Social work practice: An introduction. 4th edtiion. Basingstoke: Palgrave Macmillan.

Cournoyer, B (1991) The social work skills workbook. Belmont, CA: Wadsworth.

Crawford, K and Walker, J (2004) Social Work with older people. Exeter: Learning Matters.

Department for Education and Skills/Department of Health (2004) National Service framework for Children, Young People and Maternity Services. London, Department of Health.

Department of Health (1989) Caring for people: community care in the next decade and beyond (Cm 849). London: HMSO.

Department of Health (1991a) The Children Act guidance and regulations. Volume 2. Family support, day care and educational provision for young children. London: HMSO.

Department of Health (1991b) The Children Act guidance and regulations. Volume 3. Family placements. London: HMSO.

Department of Health (1991c) Working together under the Children Act 1989. A guide to arrangements for inter-agency co-operation for the protection of children from abuse. London: HMSO.

Department of Health (1998) Modernising social services: promoting independence, improving protection, raising standards (Cmd 4169). London: Stationery Office.

Department of Health (1999) Working together to safeguard children. A guide to inter-agency working to safeguard and promote the welfare of children. London: TSO.

Department of Health (2000a) The NHS plan: a plan for investment. A plan for reform. London: Department of Health.

Department of Health (2000b) No Secrets: guidance on developing multi-agency policies and procedures to protect vulnerable adults from abuse DOH circular HSC 2000/007. available at **www.doh.gov. uk/**

Department of Health (2001a) National service framework for older people. London: Stationery Office.

Department of Health (2001b) Fairer charging policies for home care and other non-residential Social Services – Guidance for councils with Social Services responsibilities. LAC (2001) 32. **www.doh.gov.uk/scg/homecarecharges**

Department of Health (2002a) Requirements for social work training. London: Department of Health.

Department of Health (2002b) The Single Assessment Process Guidance for Local Implementation and Annexes (HSC 2002/001; LAC (2002)). **www.dh.gov.uk/PolicyandGuidancelHealthandSocialCareTopic**s

Department of Health (2002d) Fair Access to Care Services: Policy Guidance, London, Department of Health.

Department of Health (2003a) Fair Access to Care Services Guidance on Eligibility Criteria for Adult Social Care. **www.doh.gov.uk/scg/facs**

Department of Health (2003b) Fair Access to Care Services: Practice Guidance - Implementation Questions and Answers. London, Department of Health

Department of Health (2004) Single Assessment Process for Older People, requirements for April 2004 Department of Health **www.dh.gov.uk/**

Department of Health (2005) Independence, well-being and choice: our vision for the future of social care for adults in England Cm 6499 London, Department of Health.

Department of Health (2006) Our health, our care, our say: a new direction for community services Cm 6737 Norwich, The Stationery Office.

Department of Health and Cleaver, H (2000) Assessment recording forms. London: The Stationery Office.

Department of Health, Department for Education and Employment, Home Office (2000). Framework for the assessment of children in need and their families. London: The Stationery Office.

Department of Health, Social Services Inspectorate (1995) The challenge of partnership in child protection: practice guide. London: HMSO.

Doel, M (1994) Task-centred work, in Hanvey, C and Philpot, T (eds) Practising social work. London and New York: Routledge.

Doel, M (2002) Task-centred work. In Adams, R Dominelli, L and Payne, M (eds) Social work: themes, issues and critical debates. 2nd edition. Basingstoke: Palgrave/Open University Press.

Dominelli, L (2002) Anti-oppressive social work theory and practice. Basingstoke: Palgrave.

Edlis, N (1993) Rape crisis: development of a center in an Israeli hospital. Social Work in Health Care. 18, 3/4, 169–78.

Egan, G (2001) The skilled helper: a problem-management and opportunity-development approach to helping. 7th edition. Pacific Grove: Brooks/Cole Publishing.

England, H (1986) Social work as art: making sense for good practice. London: Allen and Unwin.

Erikson, E (1950) Childhood and society. London: W.W. Norton.

Fook, J (2002) Social work: critical theory and practice. London: Sage.

Fowler, J (2003) A practitioners' tool for child protection and the assessment of parents. London: Jessica Kingsley.

Gambrill, E (1994) What's in a name? Task-centred, empirical and behavioral practice. Social Service Review, 68, 4, 578–99.

General Social Care Council (GSCC) (2002) Code of practice for employees. London: GSCC.

General Social Care Council (GSCC) (2002) Code of practice for social care workers. London: GSCC.

Gilbar, O (1991) Model for crisis intervention through group therapy for women with breast cancer, Clinical Social Work Journal, 19, 3, 293–304

Glasby, J. and Littlechild, R. (2002) Social Work and Direct Payments. Bristol: Policy Press.

Golan, N (1978) Treatment in crisis situations. New York: Free Press.

Golightly, M. (2006) Social Work and Mental Health. 2nd edition, Exeter: Learning Matters.

Gotterer, R (2001) The spiritual dimension in clinical social work practice: a client perspective. Families in Society, 82, 2, 187–93.

Griffith J (2006) Collaboration project: Single assessment process Community Care 7/9/06.

Griffiths, R (1988) Community care: agenda for action (The Griffiths Report). London: HMSO.

Harding, T and Beresford, P (1996) The standards we expect: what service users and carers want from social services workers. London: NISW.

Hartman, A (1995) Diagramatic assessment of family relationships. Families in Society, 76, 2, 111–22.

Hartmann, H (1958) Ego psychology and the problem of adaptation. New York: International University Press.

Hepworth, D, Rooney, R and Larsen, JA (1997) Direct social work practice: theory and skills. 5th edition. London: Brooks/Cole Publishing.

Hodge, D (2001) Spiritual assessment: a review of major qualitative methods and a new framework for assessing spirituality. Social Work, 46, 3, 203–14.

Hodge, D (2005) Developing a spiritual assessment toolbox: a discussion of the strengths and limitations of five different assessment methods. Health and Social Work, 30, 4, 314–23.

Horner, N (2006) What is social work? context and perspectives. 2nd edition. Exeter: Learning Matters.

Horwath, J (ed) (2001) The child's world: assessing children in need. London: Jessica Kingsley.

Howe, D (1992) An introduction to social work theory. Aldershot: Arena.

Hughes, B (1995) Older people and community care. Buckingham: Open University Press.

International Association of Schools of Social Work and International Federation of Social Workers (2001) Joint agreed definition, 27 June 2001: Copenhagen.

Johns, R (2007) Using the Law in Social Work. 3rd edition. Exeter: Learning Matters.

Joseph Rowntree Foundation (2000) Older people's definitions of quality services. York: Joseph Rowntree Foundation.

Koprowska, J (2005) Communication and Interpersonal Skills in Social Work. Exeter, Learning Matters.

Laming, H (2003) The Victoria Climbié inquiry report. Cm 5730. London: The Stationery Office.

Leece, J (2000) It's a matter of choice: making direct payments work in Staffordshire. Practice, 12, 4, 37–48.

Lewis, J and Glennerster, H (1996) Implementing the new community care. Buckingham: Open University Press.

Lindemann, E (1944) Symptomatology and management of acute grief. American Journal of Psychiatry, 101, 141–8.

Lloyd, M and Taylor, C (1995) From Hollis to the Orange Book: developing a holistic model of social work assessment in the 1990s. British Journal of Social Work, 25, 691–710.

Lymbery, M (1998) Care management and professional autonomy: the impact of community care legislation on social work with older people. British Journal of Social Work, 28, 6, 863–878.

Lymbery, M. (2005) Social Work with Older People Context, Policy and Practice. London: Sage Publications.

McCreadie, C (1996) Elder abuse: update on research. London: Age Concern Institute of Gerontology.

McDonald, A. (2006) Understanding Community Care: A guide for social workers. 2nd edition, Basingstoke: Palgrave Macmillan.

McGoldrick, M, Gerson, R and Shellenberger, S (1999) Genograms: assessment and intervention. 2nd edition. New York: Norton.

McNally, D, Cornes, M and Clough, R (2003) Implementing the single assessment process: driving change or expecting the impossible? Journal of Integrated Care. 11,2 18–29.

Mandelstam, M (1999) Community care practice and the law. London: Jessica Kingsley.

Manthorpe, J, Stanley, N, Bradley, G and Alaszewski, A (1996) Working together effectively? Assessing older people for community care services. Health Care in Later Life, 1, 3, 143–155.

Marsh, P and Doel, M (2005) The Task-Centred Book. London: Routledge.

Marsh, P and Triseliotis, J (1996) Ready to practise? Social workers and probation officers: their training and first year in work. Aldershot: Avebury.

Mayer, J and Timms, N (1970) The client speaks. London: Routledge and Kegan Paul.

Mencap (1995) Community care: Britain's other lottery. London: Mencap.

Meredith, B (1995) The community care handbook. London: Sage.

Middleton, L (1997) The art of assessment. Birmingham: Venture Press.

Milner, J and O'Byrne, P (2002) Assessment in social work. 2nd edition. Basingstoke: Palgrave.

Munro, E (1998) Understanding social work: an empirical approach. Atlantic Heights, NJ: Athlone Press.

O'Hagan, K (1991) Crisis intervention in social work, in Lishman, J (ed) Handbook of theory for practice teachers in social work. London: Jessica Kingsley, pages 138–56.

Oliver, M (1996) Understanding disability: from theory to practice. Basingstoke: Macmillan.

Olsen, MR (ed) (1984) Social work and mental health. London: Tavistock.

Olsen, S, Dudley-Brown, S and McMullen, P (2004) Case for blending pedigrees, genograms and ecomaps: nursing's contribution to the "big picture". Nursing and Health Sciences, 6, 295–308.

Orme, J (2000) Equal opportunities, in Davies M (ed) The Blackwell encyclopaedia of social work. Blackwell: Oxford.

Parker, J (1992) Crisis intervention – a framework for social work with people with dementia and their carers. Elders. The Journal of Care and Practice, 1, 4, 43–57.

Parker, J (2000) Social work with refugees and asylum seekers: a rationale for developing practice, Practice, 12, 3, 61–76.

Parker, J (2004) Effective Practice Learning in Social Work. Exeter: Learning Matters.

Parker, J (2007a) The Process of Social Work: Assessment, planning, intervention and review in M Lymbery and K. Postle (eds) Social Work: A companion for learning. London: Sage.

Parker, J. (2007b) Crisis intervention: a practice model for people who have dementia and their carers. Practice, 19, 2, forthcoming.

Parker, J and Penhale, B (1998) Forgotten people: positive approaches to dementia care. Aldershot: Ashgate/Arena.

Parker, J and Randall, P (1997) Using behavioural theories in social work. Birmingham: BASW/OLF.

Parkes, CM (1972) Psycho-social transitions: a field for study. Social Science and Medicine, 5, 101–15.

Parry, G (1990) Coping with crises. London: BPS Books/Routledge.

Payne, M (2005) Modern Social Work Theory. 3rd edition. Basingstoke: Palgrave Macmillan.

Payne, M (1995) Social Work and Community Care. Basingstoke: Palgrave Macmillan.

Perls, F, Hefferline, R and Goodman, P (1973) Gestalt therapy: excitement and growth in the human personality. Harmondsworth: Penguin.

Pierson, J (2002) Tackling social exclusion. London: Routledge.

Pincus, A and Minahan, A (1973) Social work practice. Model and method. Itasca, IL: Peacock.

Pincus, L (1976) Death and the family: the importance of mourning. London: Faber.

Postle, K (2001) The social work side is disappearing. I guess it started with us being called care managers. Practice, 13, 1, 13–26.

Postle, K (2002) Working 'between the idea and the reality': ambiguities and tensions in care managers' work. British Journal of Social Work, 32, 3, 335–52.

Quinney, A (2006) Collaborative Social Work Practice. Exeter: Learning Matters.

Ramon, S (2002) Mental wellbeing in the workplace. Professional Social Work, April, 14–15.

Rapoport, L (1970) Crisis intervention as a mode of brief treatment, in Roberts, RW and Nee, RH (eds) Theories of social casework. Chicago: Chicago University Press.

Reamer, G (1993) The philosophical foundations of social work. Columbia: Columbia University Press.

Rees, S (1991) Achieving power: practice and policy in social welfare. Sydney: Allen and Unwin.

Reid, W (1978) The task-centred system. New York: Columbia University Press.

Reid, W and Shyne, A (1969) Brief and extended casework. New York: Columbia University Press.

Reid, W and Epstein, L (1972) Task-centred casework. New York: Columbia University Press.

Richmond, M (1917) Social diagnosis. New York: Russell Sage Foundation.

Roberts, AR (ed) (1991) Contemporary perspectives on crisis intervention and prevention. Englewood Cliffs, NJ: Prentice-Hall Inc.

Roberts, AR (ed) (1995) Crisis intervention and time-limited cognitive treatment. Thousand Oaks, CA: Sage.

Rogers, C (1951) Client-centred therapy: its current practice, implications and theory. Boston: Houghton Mifflin.

Rogers, CR (1961) On becoming a person: a therapist's view of psychotherapy. London: Constable.

Royal Commission on Long Term Care (1999) With respect to old age. London: The Stationery Office.

Saleeby, D (1996) The strengths-perspective in social work practice: extensions and cautions. Social Work, 41, 3, 296–305.

Sheldon, B (1995) Cognitive-behavioural therapy. London: Routledge.

Sheppard, M, Newstead, S, DiCaccavo, A and Ryan, K (2001) Comparative hypothesis assessment and quasi triangulation as process knowledge assessment strategies in social work practice. British Journal of Social Work, 31, 6, 863–85.

147

Smale, G and Tusan, G with Biehal, N and Marsh, P (1993), Empowerment, assessment, care management and the skilled worker. London: NISW/HMSO.

Smale, G, Tuson, G and Statham, D (2000) Social work and social problems: working towards social inclusion and social change. Basingstoke: Macmillan.

Smith, G and Cantley, C (1985) Assessing health care. Buckingham: Open University Press.

Smith, J (2002) Department of Health press release. Reference 2002/0241. **www.Info.doh.gov.uk/intpress.nsf/page/2002-024111?OpenDocument**

Social Services Inspectorate (1993) Inspection of assessment and care management arrangements in social services deparments: interim overview report. London: Department of Health.

Social Services Inspectorate and Department of Health (1991a) Care management and assessment – practitioners' guide. London: HMSO.

Social Services Inspectorate and Department of Health (1991b) Care management and assessment: managers' guide. London: HMSO.

Social Services Inspectorate and Department of Health (1993) The inspection of the complaints procedures in local authority social services departments. London: Department of Health.

Sutton, C (1999) Helping families with troubled children. A preventive approach. Chichester: Wiley.

Thompson, N (2002) Anti-discriminatory practice. 3rd edition. Basingstoke: Palgrave.

Trevithick, P (2005) Social Work Skills: A practice handbook. 2nd edition. Buckingham: Open University Press.

Trotter, C (1999) Working with involuntary clients: a guide to practice. London: Sage.

Walton, RG (ed) (1986) Integrating formal and informal care – the utilization of social support networks. British Journal of Social Work, 16 (supplement).

Ward, H (ed) Looking after children: research into practice. London: HMSO.

Waterson, J (1999) Redefining community care social work: needs or risks led? Health and Social Care in the Community, 7, 4, 276–79.

Watson, D and West, J (2006) Social Work Process and Practice: Approaches, knowledge and skills. Basingstoke: Palgrave Macmillan.

Webb, S (2001) Some considerations on the validity of evidence-based practice in social work. British Journal of Social Work, 31, 1, 57–80.

Webb, S A (2006) Social Work in a Risk Society: Social and political perspectives. Basingstoke: Palgrave Macmillan.

Williams, P (2006) Social Work with People with Learning Difficulties. Exeter: Learning Matters.

Wolfensberger, W (1972) The principle of normalisation in human services. Toronto: National Institute on Mental Retardation.

Index

abuse
  use of culturagrams 54
  see also elder abuse
accidental crises 105
administrative skills in assessment 16–17
adult services
  assessment 26
    'needs led' 28
  case reviews 125–33
    process 127
    standard schedules for recording of reviews
      126
  models of intervention 104–14
  monitoring 125
  planning 71–83
    guidance and principles 71–5
    practice related issues and concepts 75–8
advocacy 112–14
  stages of 113
art
  social work as 4–5
    influence on theories and methods 85–7
ASPIRE model 8
assessment ix, 1–38
  definitional perspectives 3–8
  characteristics and features 17–18
  levels 12–13
  purposes 13–17
  types 8–11
  and care management 26–7
    eligibility criteria and fair access to services
      34–6
    'needs led' 28–9
    process 30–2
  uses with children and families 19–26
  see also financial assessment
assessment tools ix, 40–62
  culturagrams 51–5
  ecomaps 47–51
  flow diagrams and life road maps 55–60
  genograms 41–7
'assessment triangles' 20
attending 90

Baljinder, case study 53–4
Barclay Report (1982) 111
behavioural approaches to social work 93
  see also cognitive behavioural approaches

care management
  and assessment 26
    eligibility criteria and fair access to care
      services 34–6
    'needs led' 28–9
    process of 30–2
  background 27–8
  case reviews 125–33
    process 127–8
    standard schedules for recording of reviews
      126
  and models of interventions 104–14
  monitoring 125
  planning 71–82
care planning forms 75
care plans ix–x, 63–83
  in care management and adult services 71–83
    charging system 73–5
    construction 75–8
    critique 78
    grounded in reality 72
    resource constraints 72–3
    sequences and outcomes 81
    user empowerment and equal opportunities
      71–2
    within the single assessment framework 71,
      74–5
  for children in need 65–71
care plans for looked after children 66
carers
  point of view 76, 135–6
  specific assessments for 2
Carers and Disabled Children Act (2000) 76
Carers (Recognition and Services) Act (1995) 76
Caring for People (1989) 27, 111
case review and monitoring in adult services
    125–33
case reviews 122–5
case studies x
  Baljinder 53–4
  Chris 5, 7

Damien Jones *see* Damien Jones case study
Gladys Beaumont *see* Gladys Beaumont case
    study
John 4–5
Melissa Krajic *see* Melissa Krajic case study
Peter 67–8
Tony 7–8
casework evaluation 133–5
    user perspectives 135
centrality of assessment work 3
characteristics of assessments 17–18
charging for care
    users' contribution 73
    within the care plan 73–4
Charging with Care (2000) 73
child protection plans 66
child protection reviews 122
Children Act (1989) 120, 122
Children Act (1998) 19
Children Act (2004) 65
children, communication skills with 16
children and families
    assessments 19–26
        similarity to social exclusion 14
    care plans 65–71
    reviewing work with 120–5
children in need plans 65
Chris, case study 5, 7
circumplex model 43
classical conditioning 99–100
Climbié inquiry 2, 8, 63, 122
Code of ethics for social work 118, 119
Code of practice for employees xi
Code of practice for social care workers 119
cognitive behavioural approaches 98–100
    use 100–4
communication skills
    with children 14
    and construction of culturagrams 52
community care 27
    assessment of needs 30–3
    see also home–based care
Community Care Agenda for Action (1988) 27
Community care assessments 2, 24, 30–1
    and risk management 72
    targeting assessment and resources 34–5
community networking skills and radical social
        work 110–11
comprehensive assessments 32
    use of genograms 44
concepts which inform care plans 77–88
concreteness 89

conditioning, types of 99–100
confidentiality of information 16
    in care plans 70
confrontation 89
construction of subjective experiences perspective
        7–8
contact assessments 30–1
contracts 95–6
core assessments 22
core helping skills 75, 89–91
costs of care plans 72
    see also resources
crises, experience of 105
crisis intervention 107
    development 106
    multiple applications 107
    and social work 107–10
crisis theory
    development 106
    multiple applications 107
critical eligibility band 35
culturagrams 51–5
    and working with abuse 54

Damien Jones case study
    ecomap 50–1
    flow diagram 57
    genogram 46
    life road map 60
definitions of social work vii, 3–8, 88
developmental crises 105
developmental psychology 106
diagrammatic aids to assessment 40–62
dictionary definition of assessment 3
direct payments 128, 129
disability, models of 77–8
diversity in assessment 5–6
domestic violence, use of culturagrams 54

ecomaps 47–51
    construction 49–50
effectiveness 119–20
ego psychology 106
elasticity of relationships 112
elder abuse
    and risk assessment 76–7
    use of culturagrams 54
eligibility criteria 32–5
empathy 89
empirical intervention models 92–104
    cognitive behavioural approaches to practice
        98–104

task-centred practice 92–8
empirical model of social work practice, Trotter's 86
equal opportunities and care plans 71–2
evaluation
  in adult services 125–33
  and assessment 10
  of casework 133–6
  of children and families social work 120–6
  reasons for 117–20
Every Child Matters 65
evidence-based approaches to practice 4, 85–8
exchange model 15, 111
extended social work practice, comparison with short-term 93
external pressures for evaluation 119

factual knowledge 86
Fair Access to Care Services 36, 73, 128
Fairer charging policies for home care and other non-residential social services 73
families and children *see* children and families
family therapy, use of genograms 44–6
features of assessments 17–18
financial assessment of service users' means 73
flow diagrams 56–7
Forgotten people 105
formal networks 110–12
Framework for assessment of children in need and their families 19–22, 66, 123
funnel approach to levels of assessment 12

genogram interviews 47
genograms 41–7
  development of connections and relationships 43–4
  in family therapy 44–6
  symbols used 42–3
  uses 41–2
genuineness 89
gestalt therapy 106
Gladys Beaumont case study 29, 33–4
  multi-disciplinary home visit 36–8
  eligibility banding 38
  care plan 82
  case review 128–33
  and crisis intervention 108–10
goals
  agreement on 95–6
  development into tasks 96–7
Griffiths Report (1988) 27
guardianship, mental health assessments for 2

helping skills 76, 89–90
home-based care 27
  charging 73–4
hospital, mental health assessments for admission 2
human relations skills *see* interpersonal skills

immediacy 89
importance of assessment 8–9
informal support systems 111–12
initial assessments within care management 30
instrumental conditioning 100
internal pressures for evaluation 119
interpersonal skills
  in assessment 16
  for helping relationships 90–1
interventions x, 84–114
  with adults 104–13
    advocacy 112–14
    crisis theory and crisis intervention 104–10
    networking skills 110–12
  and assessment 8
  debates on theory, methods and models 85–91
  empirical intervention models 92–104
    cognitive behavioural approaches 98–104
    task-centred practice 92–8
interviews, genogram 47
issues specific assessment 9, 10

John, case study 4–5
judgements, making 5

'knowledge as process' ix
  see also process model of assessment

labelling 5–6
learning theories 98–100
  use 100–4
levels of assessment 12–13
  conceptualisation of types and 13
liaison between agencies 111
life road maps 55, 58–60
listening 91
Looking after Children forms 123
low eligibility band 36

making judgements 5
management in social services 111
Melissa Krajic case study 23–6
  care plan for Rebecca Krajic 69–70
    task-focused agreement 96
  cognitive behavioural approach 101–4

evaluation 134–5
review process 123–4
systems thinking and the use of interpersonal
skills 91
Mental Capacity Act 2005 77
mental health assessments 2
models and methods in social work
debates 85–7
evidence-based approaches 87
systems approach 88–9
moderate eligibility band 35
monitoring performance see performance
monitoring

National Occupational Standards (NOS) viii–ix
and advocacy 112–13
developing, making and writing plans 63
interventions 84
and professional development xi
reviews and the evaluation of practice 116
tools and diagrammatic aids to assessment 40
understanding assessment 1
National Service Framework (NSF) for Older
People 31
'needs led' approach
to assessment 13
in adult services 28–9
to reviewing in adult services 126
see also eligibility criteria; user empowerment
networking skills 110–11
NHS and Community Care Act (1990) 8–9, 26, 27,
30, 125
NHS Plan 31
normalisation, concept of 10, 77
nursing plans 74–5

older people, care management see care
management
operant conditioning 100
operational tasks 96
oral agreements 96
outcomes of care plans 75, 80–1
overview assessments 32

Part 8 reviews 122–5
pathway plans 66
performance monitoring
of care management 125, 127
of social work with children and families 122–3
see also evaluation
'person–centred' approach of the single
assessment process 28

person–centred approaches 106
Peter, case study 68
planning for assessment 9
plans see care plans
pluralistic evaluation 135
political model 7–8
practice knowledge 86
practice wisdom 5, 10, 134
practitioner research 134
problem–solving model 7–8
and assessment 14
association with task–centred work 93–5
process model of assessment 6, 9–10, 21
professional development and reflective practice xi
professional networking 110–11
purposes of assessment 13–17

quality of relationships 112

radical social work
and community networking skills 110–12
and strategies that promote advocacy 112
reflective practice and professional development
xi
relationships, quality and elasticity 112
Report of the Royal Commission on long term
care 73
requirements for social work education vii–ix
Requirements for social work training 85
research, importance of 134
resources
and assessments 13
and evaluation of services 119
nationally driven constraints 72–3
respondent conditioning 99–100
Review of Children's Cases regulations (1991) 121
reviews and the evaluation of practice x, 116–36
reasons 117–18
in adult services 125–33
casework evaluation 133–6
children and families 120–5
pluralistic evaluation 135
risk assessment 11
risk assessment and elder abuse 76–7
risk management
and community care assessments 72
and service users 75
road maps, life 55, 58–60

Saleeby's strengths and barriers model 14–15
SAP 33
schedules for recording of reviews in adult
services 126–7

science
  social work as 4–5
    influence on theories and methods 85–7
serious case reviews 122–5
service users
  acceptance of risk 74
  contribution to care costs 73–4
  inclusion of strengths in assessment 14–15
  participation in the assessment process 112–14
  perspectives of 135
  understanding of assessment process 13
  see also user empowerment
short-term social work practice
  comparison with extended 93
  see also crisis intervention; task-centred
    practice
single assessment process (SAP) 26, 31–3
  and care plans 71, 74–5
  critique 78
  and models of intervention 104–14
  'person-centred' approach 28
  review process 127–8
skills in assessment 16–18
SMART Planning 65
  see also interpersonal skills
social exclusion 15
social life, systems approach see systems
    approach to social life
social model of disability 77–8
social support systems
  analysing networking within 111
  importance 110
Social work and community care 78
specialist assessments 31–2
specific assessment for carers 2
spirituality 10
standard schedules for recording of reviews 126
statutory child care reviews 121
step approach to achieving goals 92, 93
stereotyping 5–6
strengths and barriers model, Saleeby's 14–15
strengths-based model of assessment 14–15
subject benchmark criteria 14
  developing, making and writing plans 63
  interventions 84

and problem-solving 94
reviews and the evaluation of practice 116
tools and diagrammatic aids to assessment 40
understanding assessment 1
substantial eligibility band 35
support systems 110–11
symbols used in developing genograms 42–3
systems approach to social life 88–9
  and crises 104–5
  links with networks and networking 111
  see also ecomaps

task-centred practice 92–8
  development 93
  importance of levels of assessment 12
  stages 92–6
theoretical knowledge 85
theories in social work
  debates 85–8
  evidence-based approaches 87
  systems approach 88–9
theory and assessment 7–8
time-specific assessment 9, 10
Tony, case study 7–8
tools, assessment see assessment tools
Trotter's empirical model of social work practice
    86
types of assessment 8 11
  conceptualisation of levels and 13
types of knowledge in social work 85–6

Understanding community care: a guide for
    social workers 78
user empowerment 112
  and care plans 71, 78
  and culturagrams 53
  see also 'needs led' assessment

values in assessment 5–6

warmth 89
Working together 122
written agreements 96